# O'BRIEN

## PEOPLE AND PLACES

by

## Hugh Weir

BALLINAKELLA PRESS

SECOND EDITION:

©1988 Hugh W. L. Weir
Ballinakella Press
Whitegate, Co. Clare, Ireland

First published 1983
Second edition 1988
ISBN 0 946538 40 9

Design: Hugh W. L. Weir
Typesetting and printing: Boethius

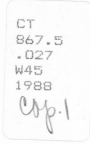

## Dedication, Preface and Acknowledgements

This little book is dedicated to the memory of Donough and Anne, whose daughter's devotion to her family is an expression of the way in which they upheld its tradition.

This second edition of *O'Brien People and Places* is an attempt to foster an interest in one of Ireland's leading families. I have tried to make it as readable and informative as possible to encourage deeper research into family history which can provide a lifetime of informative entertainment. I hope that you will enjoy it.

I must here acknowledge the tremendous help and encouragement given me by my wife Grania (née O'Brien), who did the typesetting of the first edition and supplied useful information. I would also like to mention Iseult Murphy (née O'Brien) who, together with Tom Haughey, Padraig Cleary and the Management of Shannon Development, was instrumental in developing my interest in general clan history.

I would also like to thank Topsy, my late constant canine companion, for her forbearance.

Hugh Weir

# Contents

* Illustration on following page

# Illustrations

# A Royal Heritage

O'Brien is one of the most widely dispersed and respected of Irish names. The family pedigree is amongst the oldest in Europe and goes back through Brian Boru to Milesius, the pre-Christian king of Spain, and beyond. It was due to an edict of King Brian in the eleventh century that Irish surnames first came to be used. His descendants chose his name as the basis for theirs (O'Brien means 'son of Brian'). His forebear Cas, who had twelve sons, had given his name to Brian's mid-western Dalcassian tribe.

Before his death in 1014, Brian had married at least four wives, and it is from his many children that the first family branches stem. Donough was the forebear of the Aherlow O'Briens and of those of Coonagh, near Limerick, while Teige sired another line. Six generations later Brian Ruadh (d. 1272) founded the O'Briens of Ara in Co. Tipperary. His grand-nephew's second son, Turlough the Bald, founded the Waterford branch in the late fourteenth century. whereas a generation later the Carrigogonnell O'Briens and the Dutch O'Briens were started by another younger member of this family. From Turlough Don, who died in 1528, and from his brother, Donal Baccach, stem the Ballinalacken O'Briens and those families of the senior or Royal branch, which were to hold later titles through the submission of his grandson King Murrough (the Tanaiste) to England's King Henry VIII.

There are at least seven major branches of the O'Briens which were founded before Turlough Don, and six after. Of the six later lines the senior four have become extinct, including those of the Earls of Thomond, Viscounts Clare and Marquesses of Thomond and Earls of Inchiquin. Recognised as the present main line is that of the Lemeneagh or Dromoland branch who succeeded to the title of Barons of Inchiquin in the nineteenth century. They still live in the territory inhabited by their forebears at least a thousand years ago. Early records show the Dalcassian area as being mainly the present day Co. Clare in the mid-western region of Ireland.

Nowadays O'Briens are in almost every country. In Ireland most descendants of Brian Boru still live in territories settled by their forebears centuries ago. A fascinating exercise is the location of their places. Many of their castles, abbeys, churches, houses, inaugural sites and tombs can be found. These include the magnificent Bunratty and Lemeneagh castles, Killaloe and Limerick cathedrals, Holy Cross and Corcumruagh abbeys, Birchfield and Ballycorrick houses, and the memorials such as those to Sir Donat O'Brien at Kilnasoolagh church and to William Smith O'Brien in Dublin's O'Connell Street. Some are in perfect condition and are open to the public, whereas others may be exciting mounds of stone representing castles which were destroyed in battle, such as Ballyalla near Ennis. Legends live on too; and the ghosts that haunt such places with O'Brien connections as Lemeneagh, Ballyalla, Carnelly and New Hall. In Rome one can visit the great memorial erected by Murrough of the Burnings to Brian Boru's son, King of Cashel and Thomond, Donough O'Brien, who presented his crown to Pope Alexander II before becoming a monk in the Abbey of St Stephen. In England the National Trust has opened Cliveden, the beautiful mansion which was later to become the home of Lord and Lady Astor. In Tasmania one can see where patriot William Smith O'Brien was exiled, while in Canada the pictures of nineteenth-century artist Lucius Richard O'Brien, first President of the Royal Canadian Academy, can be seen in many of the country's galleries. O'Briens contributed much to the development of the United States, and in France their chateaux and those of the families with whom they intermarried, still stand.

Contemporary members of the O'Brien family are still making a name for themselves, such as author and journalist Conor Cruise O'Brien, and best-selling author Edna O'Brien. Lord O'Brien was Governor of the Bank of England, while in Ireland other clansmen are judges, business managers, clergy, politicians and professionals. Through its development over many centuries, this family is steeped in history. For those who wish to trace the footsteps and the actions of this great Irish tribe there is a mine of rewarding research and fascinating results, for all O'Briens are heirs to an ancient and royal heritage.

# Some significant O'Brien events

| | |
|---|---|
| AD 926 | Birth of Brian Boru |
| 1002 | Brian Boru inaugurated as High King of Ireland |
| 1014 | Battle of Clontarf and death of Brian Boru |
| 1050 | Harold, future King of England, seeks Donough O'Brien's protection |
| 1101 | Royal Cashel donated to the religious by Murtagh O'Brien |
| 1192 | Anglo-Norman invasion of Thomond opposed by King Donal Mór O'Brien |
| 1277 | Brian O'Brien murdered by de Clare at Bunratty |
| 1543 | Murrough O'Brien submits to Henry VIII and becomes Earl of Thomond |
| 1605 | Donough O'Brien, fourth Earl of Thomond, becomes President of Munster |
| 1651 | Conor O'Brien of Lemeneagh dies in battle with Commonwealth forces under General Ireton |
| 1691 | William, Earl of Inchiquin, Governor of Jamaica |
| 1696 | Sir Donough O'Brien, first Baronet, moves to Dromoland |
| 1704 | Charles O'Brien, fifth Viscount Clare, made Marshal of France |
| 1741 | Death of the last O'Brien Earl of Thomond |
| 1848 | William Smith O'Brien convicted of high treason |
| 1855 | Death of the last Marquess of Thomond. Rostellan sold |
| 1873 | Marshal McMahon (O'Brien) becomes President of the French Republic |
| 1888 | Lord O'Brien ('Peter the Packer') Lord Chief Justice |
| 1897 | Birth of novelist Kate O'Brien |
| 1910 | Dermod O'Brien, President of the Royal Hibernian Academy |
| 1936 | St Patrick's Day gathering of the clan by Donough, sixteenth Baron Inchiquin |
| 1962 | Dromoland Castle sold |
| 1973 | Leslie K. O'Brien created Baron for Life |
| 1976 | Guilio Marconi's widow, Beatrice (née O'Brien) dies in Rome |
| 1977 | Grania Weir (née O'Brien) opens the Merriman Summer School on the O'Briens of Thomond: an Irish royal family |
| 1988 | Cratloe Woods opened to the public |

# O'Brien Titles of Nobility or Election

High King of Ireland
King of Munster
King of Thomond

Prince of Thomond
Prince of Cashel and Thomond

President of Munster
Governor of Munster
Governor of the Isle de France
Marshal Thomond
The O'Brien

Marquess of Billing
Marquess of Thomond
Marquis de Castelthomond

Earl of Thomond
Earl of Clare
Earl of Inchiquin
Earl of Lismore
Earl of Orkney
Compte de Thomond
Conde de O'Brien

Viscount O'Brien of Clare
Viscount Tadcaster
Viscount Tallow
Viscount Kirkwall

Baron Inchiquin
Baron Ibrikan
Baron of Castle Lyons
Baron Thomond
Baron O'Brien
Baron O'Brien of Lothbury
Baron Shannon of Cork
Baron Shandon
Baron Burren of Cork
Baron de Castelthomond

Baronet of Borris in Ossory
Baronet of Arragh
Baronet of Lemeneagh
Baronet of Ballinalacken

Knight of Calatrava
Knight of Santiago

# The O'Brien Arms

Arms were only popularly used in Ireland after the Norman invasion. It was recognised throughout Europe, however, that lions were the symbol of power and therefore of royalty. The O'Briens, descendants of High King of Ireland, Brian Boru, were amongst the first to use them. In earlier times they no doubt used primitive symbols, but from 1169 (one hundred and fifty-five years after Brian's death at Clontarf) they copied the invaders who landed in the south-east of Ireland. They painted their shields, adapted the previously used symbols and standardised their mottos. Hence they had three horizontal gold lions on a red (or crimson) background for their shield (gules, three lions passant guardant in pale or), a right arm clenching a sword for their crest (a dexter arm embowed issuing out of a cloud and brandishing a sword all proper), and the ancient Irish *Lamh Laidir in Uachtar* (the strong hand uppermost) as their motto. A second motto was later added: the French *Vigeur de Dessus*. In 1543, Murrough, King of Thomond, submitted to England's King Henry VIII, was created Earl of Thomond and permitted to retain his estates. Possibly due to his relationship with the Tudors, he was allowed to keep his royal arms with one exception. The shield was to be altered (the English royal shield was identical to the old one, consisting of three totally gold lions). The three gold lions were to be divided so that the second half was of silver (gules, three lions passant guardant in pale per pale or and argent). Murrough and his successors were also given permission to wear the royal liveries of crimson. As late as 1897 Edward O'Brien, the fourth Baron Inchiquin, attended the Jubilee celebrations of Britain's Queen Victoria by being driven by a liveried coachman and attended by a liveried servant. The arms nowadays used by the Inchiquin family are quartered (second and third respectively) so that the second quarter is 'argent, three piles meeting in point, issuing from the chief gules', and the third 'or, a pheon azure'. This shield is supported by two lions 'guardant per fesse or and argent'. Although the clan crests often differ, the arms used are almost always the three gold and silver lions.

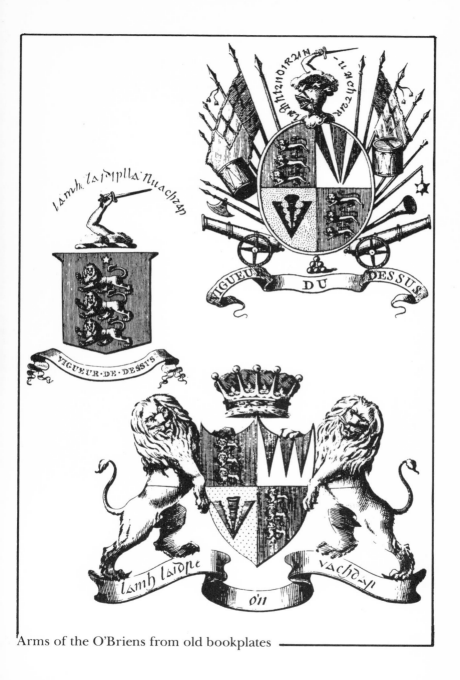

Arms of the O'Briens from old bookplates

# Brian Boru

The ancient annalists of Ireland represent Brian Boroimhe, the forefather of the Royal O'Briens from whom they take their name, as a man of fine figure and large stature, of great strength and undaunted valour; a legislator and a warrior but a king noted for his munificence, piety and patronage of the learned. Also a deeply religious man, it is said that he once spent an entire week performing acts of devotion at Armagh before offering a twenty-ounce gold collar on the high altar. Born in the north of Munster, when the Vikings were particularly active in plundering Irish monasteries and harrying the countryside, he took over chieftainship of the Dalcassians from his brother, Mathgamain, in 976. Two years later he was inaugurated King of Munster at Cashel, having slain Maelmuad who had previously held the throne. He then set his sights on Tara, the royal seat of the High Kings of Ireland. In 988 he made his way up the river Shannon waging war against the people of Connaught and the Midlands from his royal capital at Killaloe until the then King of Tara conceded the southern part of the country. But, the men of Leinster, the south-eastern province, sided with the Vikings in 999, and Brian retaliated by defeating them at Glen Mama in Co. Wicklow. Continuing to Dublin, he slayed and plundered the Viking settlement and married Gormlaith, the mother of Sitric, then King. Becoming High King himself, he made a circuit of the north to assert his superiority. Here Brian took hostages and received tributes. For this reason he was named Brian Boru, or 'Brian of the Tributes'. At the beginning of the eleventh century the Leinstermen again broke with Brian, together with the people of the north. Eventually the former got the support of the Vikings of the Orkneys and the Isle of Man who came to their assistance. A great battle was fought on Good Friday, 1014, when Brian was slain. But the Vikings were defeated and their influence on Ireland soon waned. Brian was buried at Armagh, the nation's ecclesiastical capital.

Brian Boru with his sword

# The Rock of Cashel

Often known as the Acropolis of Ireland, the massive three-hundred-foot Rock of Cashel is the site of the coronation and tribute stone, and of the royal palace of the Kings of Munster province, beside which St Patrick baptised King Aengus in 450 AD. It was here in 984 that Brian Boru, from whom the O'Briens take their name and lineage, was crowned King of Munster. He built palaces here and at Kincora (q.v.) before dying on the battlefield at Clontarf, north of Dublin, where he defeated the Danes in 1014. He had been High King of Ireland since the beginning of the eleventh century. In 1101, having gathered the chiefs and religious of the province, King Murtagh O'Brien (the last O'Brien High King) presented Cashel of the Kings to the religious of Ireland. After his death, the provincial kingdom was broken up and Cashel passed into the hands of Archbishop-King Cormac MacCarthy. He was dispossessed by Turlogh O'Brien, but regained his seat before building the chapel which bears his name in 1134. A twelfth-century cathedral was built by Donal Mór O'Brien (q.v.) who, in 1174, joined Conor O'Conor in attacking Strongbow outside the city. Marian O'Brien, Bishop of Cork, was translated to Cashel in 1224. During his fourteen years as archbishop he was granted the new town of Cashel by King Henry III. O'Brien afterwards confirmed it to a mayor and burgesses. He also licensed the nearby Lepers' Hospital, and probably reconstructed Donal Mór's cathedral. In the mid-seventeenth century, Murrough O'Brien, the first Earl of Inchiquin and President of Munster, who was known as 'Murrough of the Burnings', set fire to buildings on the Rock and massacred all therein. He was eventually granted the lands of Rostellan, Co. Cork (q.v.). The churches and buildings on the Rock were disused after the mid-eighteenth century, and still stand as magnificent ruins overlooking the fertile Golden Vale.

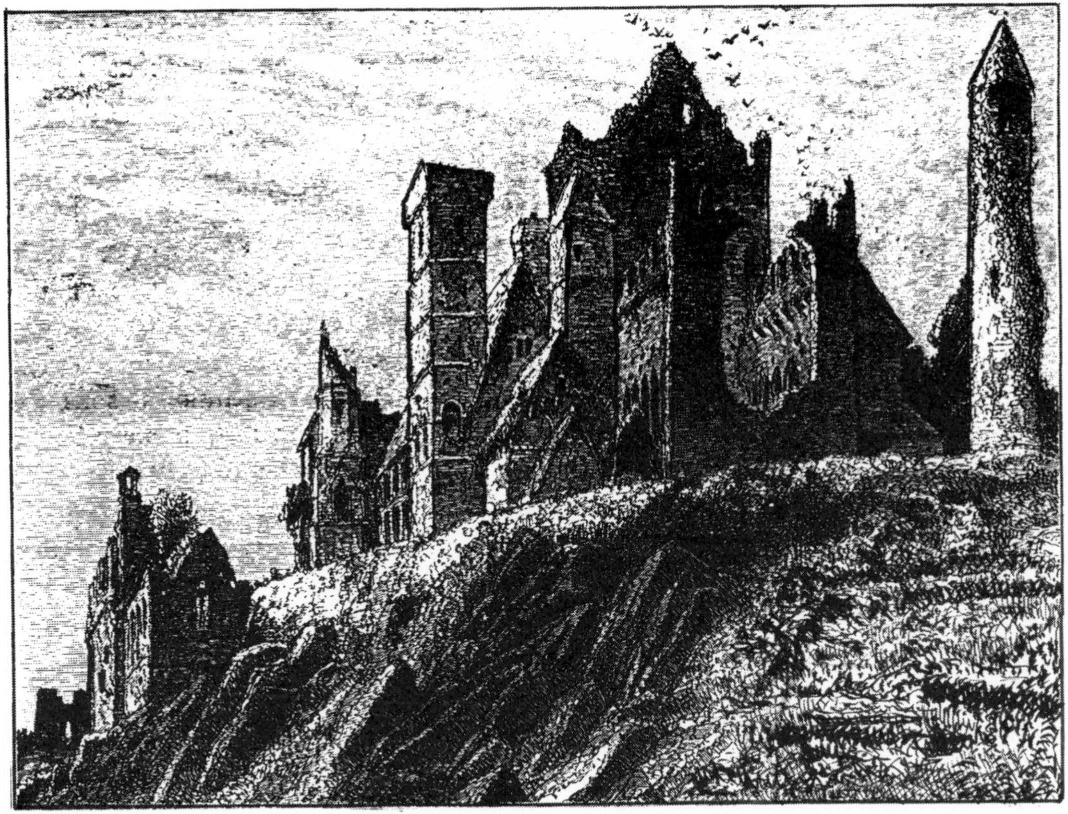

The Rock of Cashel

# Bunratty Castle

One of Shannon Development's most popular centres for visitors is Bunratty Castle, which was expertly restored in the 1960s, thanks to the munificence of Lord Gort. Built where the main Limerick to Ennis road now crosses the Owenogarney river, Bunratty stands near the site of the mid-thirteenth century Norman de Muscegros motte and bailey. Destroyed forty-five years later, the earliest stone castle was built by Thomas de Clare in 1277. Although an inscribed stone once stated that it was erected by O'Brien in 1397, the present structure was finished by Side MacConmara in the mid-1400s. It was in the hands of the O'Briens in 1500. A five-storey rectangular building, it is flanked by four square towers, each built into the corners. At either end these are linked at their heads by depressed arches. Inside, there are impressive halls, living quarters and chapels, Rinuccini, the Papal Nuncio to the Confederation of Kilkenny, had scenes from the area painted on his palace walls, having stayed here in 1646 with the Great Earl of Thomond who had restored the castle in 1617. When the 1641 rebellion broke out, the sixth Earl had built his silver plate and money worth two thousand pounds into the castle walls, and plastered it over. His servants betrayed the fact to the troops who, when they seized him, took it before his eyes. He never recovered it. His great-grandson, Henry, eighth Earl of Thomond, eventually disposed of the property to the Studdert family in 1712. They lived in the castle before moving to the house which they had constructed in 1804 on the hill above. It was then used as a constabulary barracks and an addition, later removed, was built between the two western flankers. Amongst the collection of fascinating furniture is the famous 'Armada' table, which was captured by High Sheriff Boetius Clancy from the captain's cabin of the Spanish fleet's flagship, and later presented to his brother-in-law, Conor O'Brien of Lemeneagh. It has six legs (four of them Spanish lions) and the eight-foot-long top is two inches thick.

Bunratty Castle, from the original line drawing

# Carrigogonnell Castle

Dunamase, Dunluce, Cashel and Carrigogonnell are all majestic piles surmounting significant crags. Of these Irish hilltop forts, two (Cashel and Carrigogonnell) were associated with the O'Briens. Carrigogonnell, which can be seen from most places overlooking the Shannon estuary, is situated a few kilometres from Limerick, about two kilometres from the river's south bank. Built originally by the Norman Guillaume de Breouse, or his father, on a jagged basalt rock which juts through the limestone, the castle consisted of a number of towers linked by massive ramparts. On Guillaume's exile in 1210, King John granted it to King Donough Cairbreach O'Brien for sixty marks per annum. He had paid the King homage at Waterford. Disgusted, his brothers drove him out of the castle and he took refuge at Clonroad near Ennis. Eventually Conor O'Brien, sixth in descent from the original grantee, was in residence. His descendants were known as the 'Pobble O'Briens', after the barony (Pobblebrien) on which the property is situated. Matthew O'Brien, however, broke the two-hundred-year old line of undisturbed possession when, in 1535, he surrendered to Lord Grey. The castle was eventually returned to him, but a year later its garrison of Matthew O'Brien and Desmond followers was beseiged by Lord Butler on behalf of his nephew Donough O'Brien. After heavy casualties, the fortress was committed to Lord Butler, who transferred it to Donough who was 'a scourge to the citizens of Limerick'. The latter, who plundered the neighbouring country, was deprived of the castle in 1538. By 1590, Brien Dubh O'Brien was Chieftain, but for his participation in the 1641 rebellion, Daniel O'Brien lost the property. Charles II regranted it to Archbishop Boyle of Dublin. In 1691 the castle was blown up following occupation by the Jacobites. Members of the Pobblebrien family include Murrough O'Brien, who fought at the Boyne before going to France with James II. His son, Daniel, Baron of Castle Lyons, was created Earl of Lismore (1725), Viscount Tallow (1746) by the exiled Pretender to the British throne, James III, in France. These titles expired on the death of the second Viscount in 1780. Descendants of the family still live in the immediate vicinity of this impressive ruin.

Carrigogonnell Castle, Co. Limerick

# Máire Ruadh O'Brien

Two women have each made a name in Irish legend. Grania O'Malley, the great sea captain of the Connaught coast, died around 1600 in poverty. Máire Ruadh fared better at her end. Eldest daughter of Sir Turlough and Mary (née Ryan) MacMahon of Clonderlaw, Máire married Daniel Neylon (1634) and had three sons: William of Corofin, Donal and Michael. Her grandson, Colonel Francis O'Neylon, served the German Emperor in 1733. After Daniel's death in 1639, his widow married Conor O'Brien of Lemeneagh. Her fortune was one thousand pounds. This marriage lasted thirteen years, for Conor, whom the Loyalist Lord Inchiquin appointed to raise a troop of horse in 1642, was killed by Ludlow's forces at Inchicronan nine years later. His fearless wife had accompanied him on many raids on English settlers in Clare and was prepared for any event. When Cromwell's troops confronted her with Conor's body at Lemeneagh, she denied her husband and claimed widowhood (she now was!). This enabled her to take steps to safeguard her devoted husband's estate for nine-year-old Donough. Ordering her carriage, she drove to Limerick demanding to see General Ireton. Although banqueting, he heard Máire's loud demands, reproved his guard, and bade her in. She offered to marry any one of his officers. Cornet John Cooper accepted, and the future of her property was secured. By Conor she had eight children. Donough (b. 1642) married Lucia Hamilton and was forebear of the Dromoland O'Briens. Teige married Honora FitzGerald. Honora (b. 1645) married Donough O'Brien of Duogh, and Mary became wife to Donough Macnamara. Turlough and Murrough lived, but in 1641 Mary and Slaney were buried as infants at Coad church. Mr and Mrs Cooper spent their early married days at Meelick, and possibly lived at Cratloe Castle. Their son, Henry, was probably forebear of the Clarina family. Their daughter was Mrs Wilson. Legend states that Cooper died from a kick from Máire whilst shaving, after a slight against Conor. This red-haired lady was, however, a devoted wife. Many more legends are told of Máire. She was buried either at Coad, with her infant daughters, or at Ennis Abbey.

Máire Ruadh O'Brien

# St Mary's Cathedral, Limerick

In the centre of the old city of Limerick is the medieval cathedral shrine of the Blessed Virgin. The chancel was built by Bishop Donough O'Brien at the beginning of the thirteenth century, on the site of King Donal Mór O'Brien's royal palace. Originally a cruciform building, wide side aisles were added prior to the eighteenth century, so that now the walls of the nave obtrude only a few feet beyond those of the transepts. At the west end, above the Romanesque main doorway, is a fine tower, from each corner of which rises a tall crenellated turret. Inside, one is struck by the lack of light from the many beautiful windows. St Mark's chapel formed the burial place of the Earl of Inchiquin ('Murrough of the Burnings') in 1674. He was so called from his burning down of Cashel cathedral and other churches. Legend states that the day after his burial, the Limerick people snatched his body from its coffin and threw it into the Shannon. Near the high altar is the magnificent multi-tier monument erected in 1678 by Henry, second Earl of Thomond, in memory of his grandfather, Donough O'Brien, Earl of Thomond and President of Munster, who died in 1624. It replaced the original which had been defaced by the Cromwellians, and occupied a large Gothic archway. The high altar reredos and stone surrounds were erected by the O'Briens in 1917, in memory of Captain Aubrey O'Brien, third son of Edward O'Brien of Cahermoyle. He was killed in action in 1914. The window to the south of the sanctuary is dedicated to the Hon. Robert O'Brien (d. 1870), who contributed extensively to the restoration of the church, whilst a larger one was erected for the Stafford O'Briens, as was the east window. Other monuments record such family members as Dermod O'Brien, the artist, and his brother, Dean Lucius O'Brien, and his family; and Cornelius George O'Brien, who died in 1867. An ancient stone records that the founder (1168) Donal Mór O'Brien, was buried here too. He was the first of the many O'Briens to be associated with this ancient Church of Ireland Diocesan Cathedral.

*S<sup>t</sup> Marys Cathedral*

St Mary's Cathedral, Limerick
from an early 18th century print

# Sir Donough O'Brien, First Baronet

The picture of Sir Donough (Donat) O'Brien is taken from William Kidwell's (1662-1736) magnificent monument in Kilnasoolagh church near Newmarket-on-Fergus. Born in 1645, he was the eldest son of Máire Ruadh MacMahon through her marriage with Conor O'Brien, and it was for him that she denied her marriage and offered her hand to Cromwellian officer John Cooper. Donough was then nine. Although his mother was living with Cooper in Limerick, on his twenty-first birthday he wrote to her from Lemeneagh Castle. In 1676 he married Lucia, daughter of Sir George Hamilton. Their son, Lucius, married Queen Anne's cousin, Catherine Keightly. He predeceased his father by ten months. Lucius' son continued the Dromoland branch. Lucia died in 1676. The following year, Donough married widow Elizabeth Gray, whose father was Joseph Deane of Crumlin, and whose mother a Miss Cuffe of Quin. By his second marriage he had two daughters and a son, Henry, who became the progenitor of the Stafford O'Briens. About 1685, Sir Donough moved from Lemeneagh Castle to Dromoland. The former had suffered at the hands of billeted Cromwellian troops. At the time, Dromoland was little more than a tower house, but its situation was good and the land more productive. He also built the still partly-used Sir Donat's Road, which ran east from Lemeneagh Castle. Considered by many to be the wealthiest commoner in the country, Donough was created a Baronet in 1686. Perhaps due to a legacy of war and the circumstances of his father's death, he declared himself for neither James nor William, and only captained an independent troop of twenty Dragoons for protection against 'robberies and stealths'. He was appointed a Privy Councillor of Ireland by Queen Anne, and in 1689 was made High Sheriff for Co. Clare. Well regarded by his neighbours and tenants, he was a conformist to the established Church of Ireland. He endowed the local school at Newmarket-on-Fergus, and presented a fine silver chalice and patten for use in Kilnasoolagh church. He died in 1717. His second son, Henry, organised the erection of his memorial.

Sir Donough O'Brien

# Lemeneagh Castle

Above a bend on the road between Corofin and Kilfenora, in the Clare countryside, one is confronted with the splendid spectacle of Lemeneagh Castle, Facing the front, one can distinguish the original fifteenth-century tower house on the right. To this was added the magnificent four storey, four bay, fortified mansion, with its mullioned windows and protective eyebrows. This stone house was, according to the inscription on the arched gateway which was moved and reconstructed at the entrance to Dromoland's walled garden, completed by Conor and Máire (ni Mahon) O'Brien in 1643. At one time it was surrounded by extensive wooded parklands. In the valley to the east one can still locate part of the original stable block where Máire (Ruadh) O'Brien kept her famous stallion. In the gable wall two niches were built for the grooms to take cover from his ferocity. Sir Donat's (O'Brien) road runs for many miles to the east and was probably built by Conor and Máire's son, the first Baronet, to facilitate transport between the castle and his new house at Dromoland. The walls of the deerpark which supplied venison are still to be seen about half a kilometre to the north-east. During the Cromwellian occupation, Commonwealth troops moved in, and the O'Briens sojourned in nearby Inchiquin Castle, where they had previously lived. When the soldiers left, the trees had been cut down for firing, the deerpark decimated, and the house in such appalling condition that in about 1686 Sir Donough (Donat) O'Brien decided to move to his estate at Dromoland. In the early twentieth century, Sir Lucius O'Brien, fifteenth Baron, transferred to Dromoland the gateway which stood in a high wall a short distance from the front door, together with a fine stone fireplace. In 1962, the latter was moved to the Old Ground Hotel in Ennis, where it was incorporated in the walls of an early fortified town house. Only fully inhabited by the O'Briens for less than half a century, Lemeneagh was reputedly occupied until the end of the 1700s. Now it is a majestic ruin.

Lemeneagh Castle from an old drawing

# William, Fourth Earl of Inchiquin

One of the great figures of the eighteenth century, William O'Brien, fourth Earl of Inchiquin in the Peerage of Ireland, Baron of Inchiquin, and Baron of Burren, was born at Rostellan, Co. Cork, in 1694. His father, who died in 1719, had married Margaret O'Brien, who died in 1688. William's mother was his second wife, Mary, daughter of Sir Edward Villiers. The year after succeeding to the title, the fourth Earl married Lady Anne Hamilton, daughter of the first Earl of Orkney. Tragedy struck them with the successive deaths of their four sons. William and George both died when one year old, Augustus died an infant, and Murrough, Lord O'Brien, the fourth son, died of smallpox in 1741 when he was ten years old. As his mother became Countess of Orkney in her own right, he was Viscount Kirkwall, and was to have also succeeded the eighth and last Earl of Thomond, who had no heir. They both died in the same year, so this extensive property went to his wife's nephew, Percy Wyndham. After Anne's death in 1756, the Earl of Inchiquin married Mary, daughter of Viscount Mount Cashel, who lived her last years in Dublin's Kildare Street. Heiress to William and the Countess of Orkney's magnificent house and demesne at Cliveden, in Buckinghamshire, was their eldest daughter, the deaf and dumb Mary. She married her first cousin, the first Marquess of Thomond. Their daughter's line continued the Scottish earldom. William represented the English borough of New Windsor in the Parliaments of 1715 and 1722, Camelford in 1741, and Aylesbury, Buckinghamshire, in 1747. Immediately after the re-establishment of the honour by King George I in 1725, he was made a Knight Companion of the Bath, and in 1744 was Lord of the Bedchamber to Frederick, Prince of Wales. On the death of his kinsman, the Earl of Thomond, in 1741, he was made Governor of County Clare. Lord Inchiquin was also elected Masonic Grand Master in 1727. He died in July 1777, and was buried near his father at the small East Cork Cathedral, close to his family home at Rostellan.

William, Fourth Earl of Inchiquin

# Rostellan, Co. Cork

In 1664, Murrough ('of the Burnings') O'Brien, first Earl of Inchiquin, whose mother was Ellen Fitzgerald of nearby Cloyne, was granted the estate of ten thousand acres he had previously captured at Rostellan, in Co. Cork. Here he took over the Fitzgerald castle where, in 1691, his eldest son William, the second Earl, died. William's eldest son, also called William, was one time Governor of Jamaica. His grandson William, the fourth Earl, built the first house round the castle, and married Anne Hamilton, Countess of Orkney. Her home was Cliveden, near Taplow, which became O'Brien property. In recent years it became the property of Lord and Lady Astor. Murrough, the fifth Earl, Knight of St Patrick, and Privy Councillor, married his cousin, Lady Mary O'Brien, and secondly, Mary Palmer, who, as niece of Sir Joshua Reynolds (d. 1792) inherited forty thousand pounds including his studio of pictures. The last member of the O'Brien family to live here was James, the seventh Earl and third Marquess of Thomond. An admiral, he commanded the *Emerald* at the capture of St Lucia and Surinam. On his death in 1855, these O'Briens, the marquisate, and the earldom became extinct, for he had no male heirs by his two wives. Legend had it that, during the construction of the mid-eighteenth century house, an old graveyard was disturbed. A local woman, whose family were buried there, cursed that the Earl would never have a direct heir. The fourth Earl and his titled successors had no sons. Murrough, the fifth Earl, further improved the house around 1780, to which his nephew added when he succeeded in the early nineteenth century. The three-storey house, demolished in 1944, was situated on a peninsula jutting out from the east side of Cork harbour. It was approached by a long drive, and was adjoined by a mock medieval yard. A fine family coat-of-arms carved in stone surmounted the front door, and is now in the Cork Municipal Museum.

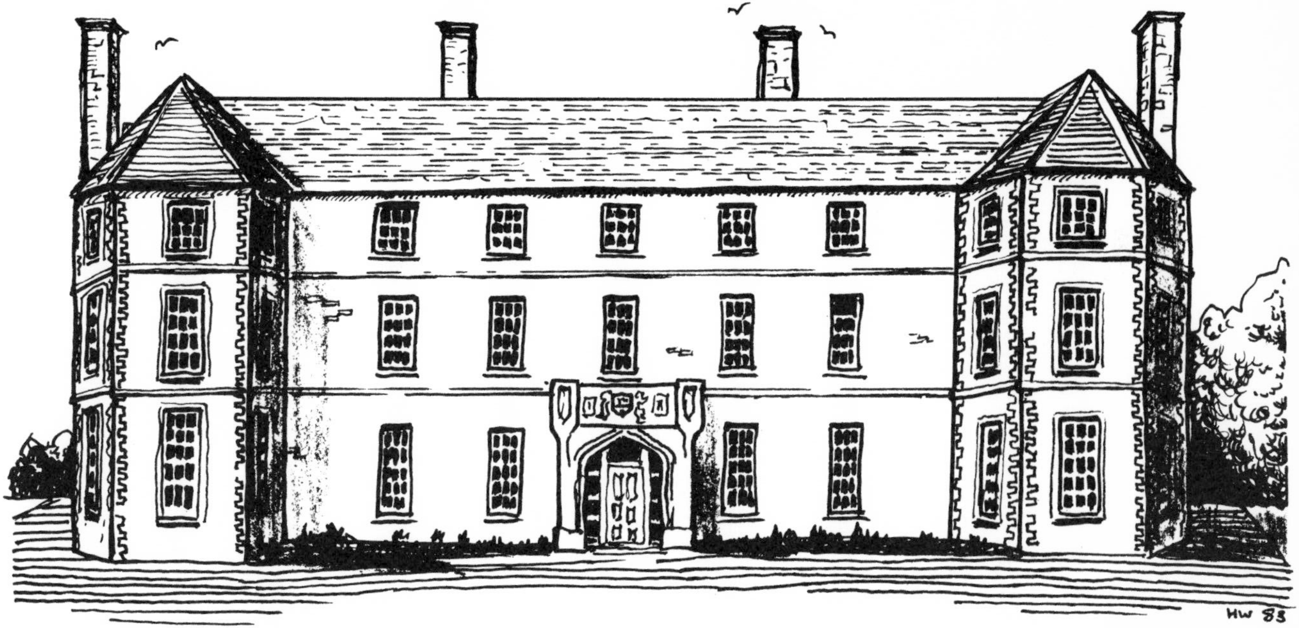
HW 83

Rostellan, Co. Cork

# Sir Lucius O'Brien, third Baronet

Sir Lucius Henry O'Brien was born at Dromoland in 1731. When sixteen years old he entered Dublin's Trinity College and became a scholar of Latin and Greek, and four years later, a B.A. Vernon. By 1728, he had been called to the Irish Bar. It was not long before he entered parliament as the member for Ennis, for in 1763 he spoke on conditions in Co. Clare with such deep sincerity and concern that Lecky quoted his speech in his *History of England*. Sir Lucius spent thirty years as a politician. During this time his friendship with Clare-born patriot Charles Lucas encouraged him to become a prominent member of the popular party. An inarticulate but clever debater and keen on commerce he endeavoured to have trade restrictions between Great Britain and Ireland removed. He also headed the Clare Volunteers, and was active in efforts for Irish legislative independence; in 1782 he supported Grattan's motion for an address to the King in its favour. Five years later, whilst member of parliament for Tuam, having lost his Clare seat, he was made a member of the Privy Council, and appointed clerk to the Crown and Hanaper in the High Court of Chancery. Sir Lucius was one of nine children and succeeded his father, Edward, as third Baronet in 1765. His mother, Mary, was a daughter of Hugh Hickman of nearby Fenloe, who had been married in 1726. In 1768, Sir Lucius wedded Anne, daughter of Robert French of Monivea in Co. Galway. They had six sons and eight daughters. Their eldest son, Edward, who was born in 1773, became the fourth Baronet; Robert became an admiral; Nichola married relative Robert French of Monivea; Anna Maria married Archdeacon Spooner (of spoonerism fame), and Charlotte married the first Earl of Gainsborough's brother. Although at different times representing Ennis, Clare and Tuam in parliament, Sir Lucius was able to cultivate hemp and lucerne at Dromoland. He worked hard with such projects as the development of Shannon navigation, and was an active member of the Church of Ireland. This scholar, lawyer, economist and parliamentarian died at Dromoland on 15 January 1795.

Sir Lucius O'Brien

# Dromoland Castle

The early nineteenth-century mansion now standing on the 'Hill of Litigation' succeeds an earlier classical house. In 1599, Murrough O'Brien (the Tanaiste) gave Donough, his third son, Lemeneagh and Dromoland. His descendants lived on this site until Donough O'Brien, the sixteenth Baron Inchiquin, was financially compelled to sell in 1962. After Cromwell had ransacked Lemeneagh in the late seventeenth century, Donough's great-great-grandson, the first Baronet, moved the family seat to Dromoland. Fifty years later, a delightful ten bay, two-and-a-half storey house over a basement, with a pedimented, four bay breakfront facing over the lake was erected, possibly to the design of John Aheron. The central front door, approached by seventeen steps, was at the rear. To the south was a two storey quadrangle completed in 1736. In the early nineteenth century Sir Edward O'Brien, fourth Baronet, decided to rebuild. The Pain brothers were commissioned, and submitted pleasant classical designs, but Sir Edward chose the style introduced by John Nash. This was the neo-Gothic used at nearby Lough Cutra Castle, the building of which was supervised by Nash's pupils, James and George Pain. Dromoland consists of four linked, irregular, castellated turrets. To the north front is attached a Gothic porch incorporating the O'Brien arms. The west prospect faces over the lake, and the east towards the hill on which the sixteenth Baron built Thomond House in 1965. To the south are the large walled gardens entered through the Lemeneagh gateway, whilst between them and the house are the main yards. The house is approached by a curving drive from the imposing gateway and its classical lodge. This passes north of the lake and used to hook round to the front door. Now the main entrance is through a new edifice built in the original style, which is situated in the south-east wall. The porch faced the classical temple reputedly built over the grave of Sir Edward O'Brien's (second Baronet) favourite horse, and the magnificently laid out wooded landscape with its long walks and vistas. Across the road from the main entrance gate is the turret built for observing horses being trained, and which was depicted on a recent Irish postage stamp. Dromoland Castle is now a high-grade hotel.

Dromoland Castle, Co. Clare

# Jockey Hall, Co. Kildare

Sir Edward O'Brien, the second Baronet, of Dromoland, was twelve years old when, on 17 November 1717, he inherited his title and estates from his grandfather, Donough, only ten months after the death of his father, Lucius. His mother, Catherine Keightly, was first cousin to both Queens Mary and Anne, and it was not long before Edward started living 'royally' by participating in such expensive activities as racing at Newmarket. He kept a fine stable of horses and was responsible for getting John Aheron to design the hilltop turret opposite the gates of Dromoland so that he could watch them racing. This building, which was depicted on an International Architectural Heritage Year postage stamp, was furnished and hung with racing pictures. Sir Edward, who also kept his own pack of hounds, married Mary Hickman of Fenloe when he was twenty-one. She did not approve of his activities, and legend has it that she destroyed his racing records before her death in 1760. He died five years later, a much poorer man than he would have been had his kinsman Henry, the last Earl of Thomond, included him in his Will. It seems that Edward's extravagant life style helped the latter decide that he was not a suitable heir, so his estate eventually passed through his connection, Percy Wyndham, to Lord Leconfield. Amongst Sir Edward's close friends were the Quins of Adare, forebears of the Earls of Dunraven, who were no doubt entertained at his racing lodge on the Curragh. Jockey Hall, for some time an excellent restaurant, was built facing a small hill from the north-east of the common. Behind it is good farmland. It consists of a low, seven bay, single storey house, with a central front door protected by a hexagonal porch with niches. At each end of the centre are half-hipped, two storey, three bay long wings at right angles, the front single bay of each of which juts forward. To the north-east there are large blocks of half-hipped, two storey stables and barns, and in front, between them and the house, are two handsome gate piers with half-domed, grooved capstones, and cast iron railings. The magnificent mature beech trees are probably as old as the house.

Jockey Hall, the front facing the Curragh

# Edward Donough, fourteenth Baron Inchiquin

The illustration of Edward Donough O'Brien, fourteenth Baron Inchiquin, is taken from a drawing done in 1897 by the famous Florence-born American portrait artist, John S. Sargent, R.A. It is a sketch for one of a series of paintings he executed of members of the Government side of the House of Lords to celebrate the sixtieth year of Queen Victoria's reign. Born in 1839, Lord Inchiquin was the eldest son of Sir Lucius O'Brien who claimed his right to the Barony. This was confirmed by the Committee of Privileges of the House of Lords in 1862. His mother was Mary, eldest daughter of William FitzGerald of Adelphi, near Corofin. Edward Donough was educated at St Columba's College, Dublin, with four of his cousins, and at Trinity College, Cambridge, where he obtained his M.A. Around 1860, being in poor health, he visited Greece and Egypt. His party was armed, and the tales of his travels are particularly interesting. In 1862 he was High Sheriff for Co. Clare. He married the Hon. Emily Holmes à Court, second daughter of the second Baron Heytesbury, whose father was the Lord Lieutenant of Ireland from 1844 to 1846. They had three sons and a daughter. She died six years later and, in 1874, Lord Inchiquin married the Hon. Ellen Harriet White, eldest daughter of Lord Annaly, K.P., of Luttrelstown, Co. Dublin. She was the mother of his three further sons and seven daughters, and outlived him by thirteen years. A Knight of St Patrick, active Chairman of the Ennis Board of Guardians, and Lord Lieutenant for Co. Clare, Lord Inchiquin was also Honorary Colonel of the 7th Brigade of the Southern Irish Division of the Royal Artillery. As a representative peer in the House of Lords, he constantly attended to his duties, and frequently involved himself in debates on Irish affairs. He died at Dromoland Castle in 1900 whilst Queen Victoria was visiting Ireland, and was succeeded by his eldest son, the thirty-five year old Lucius William O'Brien, who had been born in 1864, and who became a member of the Irish Senate in 1921.

Edward Donough, Fourteenth Baron Inchiquin

# Castletown Manor

To the west of Enniskillen, county town of Fermanagh in the north of Ireland, Castletown Manor is now owned by Dr Richard Brandon, whose forebear, John Brien, purchased it in 1790. These O'Briens were an important Cavan and Leitrim family who possibly arrived in that area from Thomond in the sixteenth century. John's great-grandfather was the Reverend Andrew Hamilton, a distant relative of Malcolm Hamilton, Archbishop of Cashel, who was granted the manor in the early seventeenth century. The O'Briens then had many links with the Hamiltons. The fourth Earl of Inchiquin married Anne Hamilton, Countess of Orkney, in 1720, and Sir Donough O'Brien, first Baronet, married Lucia, daughter of Sir George Hamilton of Nenagh. Malcolm built the magnificent Monea Castle on the site of the earlier Maguire fortress, overlooking their original lake dwelling. Although much of the bawn was removed by the related Weirs of nearby Hall Craig in the eighteenth century and used for the reconstruction of their demesne, most of the castle itself still stands, thanks to the efforts of the Reverend W. S. Steele and the Northern Ireland government. It had been burnt down in the mid-1700s, after which a new house on the hill above was built. The fine two storey manor house, with its three bay front and central main door approached by a flight of steps, was built in 1869 by John Dawson Brien, D.L., in whose memory the nearby twentieth-century church of St Molaise was erected. He was the grandson of the original purchaser. His father, who had married Charlotte, daughter and co-heir of the Reverend William Dawson, was High Sheriff of Fermanagh in 1839. Although he had married Frances, daughter of Captain William Smyth, whose family had previously owned the estate, John Dawson Brien had no heirs. Of his four sisters, Wilhelmina Ruth married Robert Weir, J.P., of Hall Craig; Charlotte married a Dubliner; Mary married Henry Braddell, J.P., and Rosanna, the eldest, married the Reverend Loftus Reade. Their family succeeded to the property. Their granddaughter, Elinor Brien Steele, who died at the end of the 1970s aged ninety-nine, left Castletown and its well-wooded demesne to the present owner.

Castletown, Co. Fermanagh

# William Smith O'Brien

At the top of Dublin's O'Connell Street is a monument to the great nineteenth-century nationalist patriot, William Smith O'Brien. The second son of Sir Edward O'Brien, the fourth Baronet, of Dromoland Castle, he inherited his mother's family estate at Cahermoyle (q.v.). Charlotte, the eldest daughter and co-heiress of William Smith, had married Sir Edward in 1799. Born in 1803, William Smith O'Brien, who married Lucy Caroline Gabbett when he was twenty-nine, had been educated at Harrow and at Cambridge. In 1826 he was elected Conservative member of parliament for Ennis, and from 1826-43 he represented Limerick. His parliamentary experience, however, changed his views. Originally a Protestant 'country gentleman' of conservative politics, with a liberal and practical slant, he opposed the Irish Arms Act of 1843, and became an ardent supporter of Catholic emancipation. With the help of Gavan Duffy, this leading member of the Young Irelanders, which had been founded in 1846, quitted the old Repeal Association and founded the Irish 'Confederation'. Then a pacifist, he succeeded in having the militant members out-voted and they retired. O'Connell's repealers strongly opposed the whole Young Ireland movement, and although he drew no distinctions, in 1845 Lord Clarendon had O'Brien, Meagher and Mitchel arrested for seditious writing and speaking. Mitchel was convicted and transported. This expedited the party's resort to arms, and at a rising which was prepared at Ballingarry in Co. Tipperary, O'Brien and his party clashed with the police in the widow McCormack's cabbage garden. His forces melted away, leaving him to be arrested and sentenced to death at nearby Thurles. This sentence was commuted to transportation to Tasmania. In 1854 he was freed on condition that he did not return to the United Kingdom. He lived with his family in Brussels, where he wrote *Principals of Government or Meditations in Exile*, which was published in 1856. Two years later he was fully pardoned and returned to Ireland, where he contributed to the *Nation*. He took no further part in politics. His health failed and he died at Bangor in Wales in 1864. His body was brought to Dublin five days later, where there were scenes of nationalist demonstration. He was buried at Rathronan, Co. Limerick.

William Smith O'Brien

# Cahermoyle

On the 12 November 1799, Charlotte Smith married Sir Edward O'Brien, the fourth Baronet, of Dromoland. Because she was the eldest daughter and co-heir of William Smith, Cahermoyle became the property of her son, William Smith O'Brien, the patriot (q.v.), who had assumed the additional name of Smith on the death of his maternal grandfather. His eldest son by his wife Lucy Caroline Gabbett, was Edward William O'Brien. Born in Limerick in 1837, he died in London aged seventy-one. Edward's second child was his eldest son, William Dermod O'Brien, the well-known artist, who was elected President of the Royal Hibernian Academy in May 1910. His five children by his wife Mabel Emmeline, second daughter of surgeon Sir Philip Crampton Smyly, were the last members of the family to have been brought up on the estate.

Situated less than a mile to the north-east of the pleasant west Co. Limerick village of Ardagh, near Newcastlewest, the present house was built in the early 1870s to the design of Pugin's disciple, the famous church architect J. J. McCarthy. He was responsible for such magnificent works as St Macartan's Cathedral, Monaghan; Thurles Cathedral; St Eugene's Cathedral, Derry, and the finishing of Killarney and Armagh's Roman Catholic cathedrals. Edward O'Brien was prepared to commission the best of his day, and erected the new two storey, three bay house of coursed rough-hewn stone in Celto-Romanesque revival style. The round arched windows and doorways are highlighted by carved grey and white stone supported by pink marble columns. The hipped roof is supported by a stone arcaded cornice, and on one side of the house there is a three storey tower. On another is a large balustraded porch. The two storey hall is embellished with carvings of figures and foliage, and the fireplaces are created from multicoloured marble from different parts of Ireland. In 1878, U. H. Hussey de Burgh records Edward William O'Brien of Cahermoyle as owning a total of 4990 acres with a rateable valuation of £3,630. Cahermoyle is now in the hands of a religious order who no doubt particularly respect the ecclesiastical style of its architect.

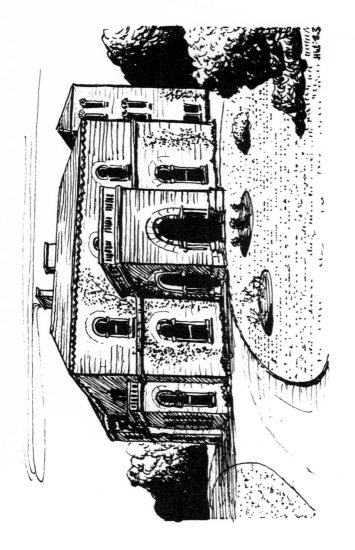

Cahermoyle, Co. Limerick

# Charlotte Grace O'Brien

The second daughter of patriot William Smith O'Brien by his wife Lucy Caroline Gabbett, was Charlotte Grace O'Brien, who made for herself a name as a leading author and social reformer and worker. She was born at Cahermoyle during the great famine in 1845. This may well have influenced her, for in her early years she witnessed many of the appalling circumstances of the times. When she was three years old, her father was transported to Tasmania and only returned eight years later when she was eleven. She was therefore reared to be a rebel. By the time she was twenty-three she had written a rousing novel on the Fenian Rising of 1869. *Light and Shade* was based on the stories and information she had gathered from her father's friends, and from other leaders of the movement. When her father died in 1864, Charlotte continued to live at Cahermoyle with her eldest brother, Edward, and his wife. After fifteen years she left Cahermoyle and went to reside at Foynes, spending the rest of her life there. Here too she wrote her first book of poetry, *Drama and Lyrics*, and an article, 'The Irish Poor Man', which was published in the *Nineteenth Century* magazine. A strong supporter of parliamentarian Charles Stewart Parnell, she became intensely concerned with the conditions of the poor and of the plight of the emigrants to the New World. She perpetually wrote to magazines and newspapers to highlight the appalling conditions at New York and at Queenstown (Cobh), where she set up a reasonably priced and well kept hostel. She travelled to England, where she inspected conditions on the vessels, and was influential towards their improvement, and to America, where she succeeded in getting better hostel accommodation for new arrivals. At Foynes she wrote several more books, including *Cahermoyle — or the Old Home*, in 1886, and was an early instigator of the 'buy Irish' campaign. She became an Irish language enthusiast, and a member of the Gaelic League, and worked hard for the revival of Irish industry. A keen botanist, she was a correspondent of a gardening magazine. Although brought up in the Church of Ireland, she died a Roman Catholic in 1909, and was buried overlooking her beloved Foynes.

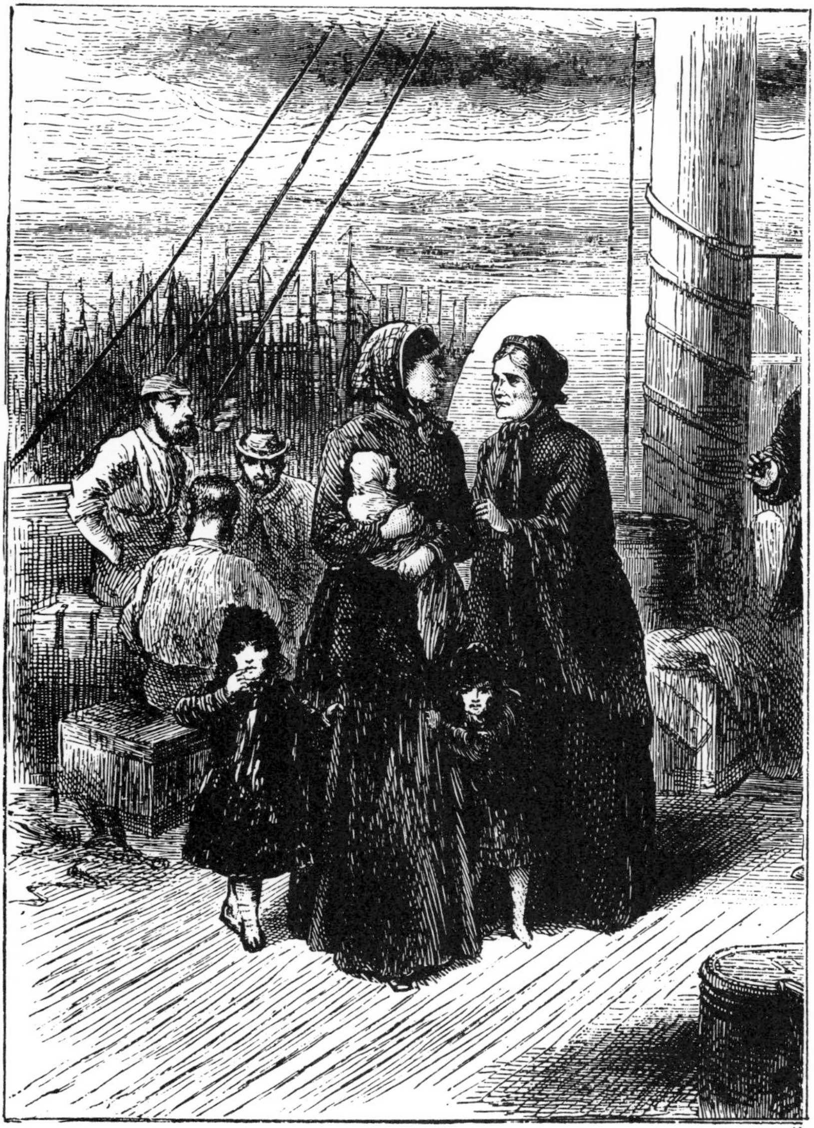

The emigration ship

# The Sixteenth Baron and Baroness Inchiquin

Sir Donough Edward Foster O'Brien, sixteenth Baron Inchiquin, was born in 1897, and educated at Eton, Sandhurst, and Magdalen College, Oxford. Having joined the Rifle Brigade when aged nineteen, he saw active service and was wounded during World War I. In 1919 he became aide-de-camp to the first Viscount Chelmsford, Viceroy of India. During this period he was honoured with the Order of the Crown of Roumania by that country's Crown Prince. He married Lord Chelmsford's daughter, the Hon. Anne (Molyneux) Thesiger, in 1921. During the early twentieth century Irish Revolution, participants suggested that he would head a restored monarchy, but this idea was dropped in favour of a republic. Donough succeeded his father as Baron whilst working as a London furrier in 1929. After the death of his mother in 1940, he got permanent army leave to return to Dromoland, where the Irish army was billeted during the emergency. He succeeded in making the estate viable, and from 1948 organised American paying guests for the castle. For promoting Irish-American friendship, he received honorary citizenship of New Orleans from the city's Mayor in 1956. Due to rising costs, he was forced to sell the castle and three hundred and fifty acres in 1962. He erected Thomond House on the hill above, and continued farming the remaining 1,250 acres. He became active in forestry, the Church of Ireland's General Synod, in lifeboat, agricultural and other organisations. He died at Ennis in 1968. Lady Inchiquin, Lord Chelmsford's second daughter, was a cousin of Sir Winston Churchill and of U.S. Ambassador to Ireland, Raymond Guest. Her mother, the Hon. Frances Guest, was Lord Wimborne's eldest daughter. Born in 1898, she organised the gardens and guesthouse at Dromoland. She lectured in America on Irish homes and their families, and was Diocesan President of the Mothers' Union before her death at Newmarket-on-Fergus in 1973. She was buried beside her husband in the family vault. They had two daughters, Deirdre and Grania, but, for the first time in the history of the Dromoland branch, no direct male heir. Lord Inchiquin's brother then took on the title.

The Sixteenth Baron & Baroness Inchiquin,

# O'Brien Miscellanea

**Allegorical Painting**
In St Criacomino's church in Rome is an interesting allegorical painting of Donough O'Brien, King of Cashel and Thomond, presenting his sceptre to St Patrick when he gave the crown and regalia to the Pope in the eleventh century.

**Bog Oak Panels**
After her death in 1874, the last Marchioness of Thomond left the thirteenth Baron Inchiquin four pictures painted on bog oak tablets depicting scenes from the life of Brian Boru. These historically valuable paintings are of significant national importance.

**Brian Boru's Banner**
Blue and gold were the colours reputedly carried by Brian Boru at the Battle of Clontarf in 1014. They are now used by such organisations as the G.A.A. as representing Co. Clare, the ancient territory of the O'Briens, on their banners and flags. They were also used by the Newmarket-on-Fergus National School's guard of honour at the author's marriage to the Hon. Grania O'Brien at Kilnasoolagh church in 1973.

**Brian Boru's Dam**
From Kincora to the waters' edge there stretches a man-made mound. Legend relates that Brian Boru was troubled by a rival's activities bordering the upper Shannon and decided to raise the level several metres by damming the river. War and the force of the water prevented completion of the scheme, but remains of the part he started can still be seen.

**Brian Boru's Ring**
A large solid gold ring reputed to have belonged to Brian Boru has been passed down through each senior family member. There is no record of how it came into their possession, and experts believe that it is, in fact, of later date.

**Conor O'Brien's Sword**
The sword used by Conor O'Brien of Lemeneagh Castle when he was fatally wounded fighting Cromwellian forces was a heavy hand-forged weapon which needed two hands to wield. It is still in family hands.

**Ghosts**
'A pleasant little old lady' was often seen on the stairs at Ballyalla, while Máire Ruadh is supposed to haunt the drive at Carnelly, near

Clarecastle. Adelphi, above Corofin, which has strong O'Brien connections, was haunted by a member of the FitzGerald family with whom they intermarried.

## 'Hobson's Choice'
Two daughters of Timothy O'Brien of The Crescent, Limerick, Emma M. and Mary Jane, were equally beautiful. Emma married Mr Hobson, who had found difficulty in which to choose as his wife.

## Inchiquin Reel and Brian Boru's March
These two traditional tunes are often played, especially in Co. Clare. *Lord Clare's Dragoons* and the *Lament for Annie O'Brien* are others.

## Inchiquin Vault
Outside the north-east corner of Kilnasoolagh church is a magnificent hip-roofed stone vault, where the last to be interred were Donough, sixteenth Baron Inchiquin (d. 1968) and his wife Anne (d. 1973), daughter of Viscount Chelmsford. Previously the bodies of the Hon. Robert O'Brien (d. 1870) and his brother, the thirteenth Baron (d. 1872), had been the sole occupants.

## Liscannor Column
The tall pillar which stands beside Liscannor Holy Well, overlooking his house at Birchfield, was erected as a memorial to the philanthropic actions of Cornelius O'Brien, M.P., during the early nineteenth century.

## Moghaun Gold Find
Whilst constructing the Ennis to Limerick railway in 1854, workmen discovered, through the glint in the pond water, a huge find of Bronze Age (twelfth to ninth century B.C.) gold objects. Some were brought to Dromoland, whilst many were melted down. Thirteen are preserved in the National Museum in Dublin, and the same number in the British Museum in London. Moghaun's vast ring fort is encompassed by the walls of Dromoland.

## Motor Vehicles
Amongst the early cars owned by the O'Briens were the eleventh to be registered in Co. Clare (IE 11), De Dions, and a 1913 thirty horsepower Napier in the scarlet and silver livery, which is now in Britain's Caister Castle Museum, Norfolk, having remained at Dromoland until the middle of the twentieth century.

## Newmarket Trowel
Presented to the Ennis Museum by the sixteenth Baron Inchiquin,

this inscribed silver trowel with its ivory handle was given to E. O'Brien Esq. as a token of respect by the Teetotallers of Newmarket-on-Fergus on 25 March 1840, after the building of Dromoland Castle.

## O'Brien Knot
Used by the Dromoland branch of the family, the O'Brien knot, which can be seen on the Lemeneagh fireplace in Ennis, is a square of intertwined single-threaded rope. Its origins are unknown, but it was no doubt based on an early Celtic design.

## O'Brien Pedigree
A tremendous pedigree linking the O'Briens with Adam, which is written on ten metres of parchment, is now preserved in the National Library, where Donough O'Brien, sixteenth Baron Inchiquin, placed it for safe keeping after the sale of Dromoland Castle in 1962.

## O'Brien Seal Matrixes
Amongst the many seal matrixes recorded as being extant in public and private hands are those of Donachadta ni Brien, which depicts a sailing vessel and two fishes, and which belonged to a fourteenth-century member of an Atlantic shore O'Brien, and of Brian O'Brien, which is of silver and depicts a griffin. It is approximately three centimetres in diameter.

## Smith O'Brien Gold Cup
This cup, now in the National Museum of Ireland, was presented to William Smith O'Brien by fellow-countrymen in Melbourne after his release from prison in 1854. About half a metre high, it was made by Mr Hackett of that Australian city. Its symbolism links the two countries most associated with the patriot.

## Sword of Brian Boru
Acquired by the Vernon family of Clontarf from the estate of the last Marchioness of Thomond, who died in 1874, this heavy sword was, according to Croker in his *Researches in the South of Ireland*, at Rostellan in 1813. Almost two metres long, it needed two hands to wield. (See the illustration of Brian Boru in this book).

## Thomond Diamonds
In 1874, the Marchioness of Thomond left a magnificent diamond necklace/tiara and drop earrings to Lucius, thirteenth Baron Inchiquin. Now kept in a bank vault, they are known as 'the Thomond diamonds', and have been passed down since then to each holder of the Inchiquin title.

# IRELAND

## MAIN O'BRIEN AREAS

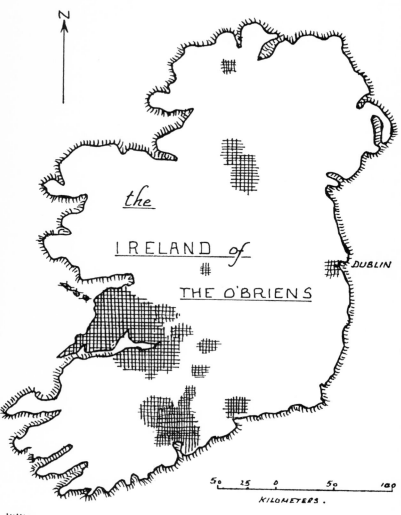

the

IRELAND of

THE O'BRIENS

DUBLIN

N

50   25   0        50        100

KILOMETERS.

▦ major O'Brien localities.                    H.W. 83.

# IRELAND

## SIGNIFICANT O'BRIEN PLACES

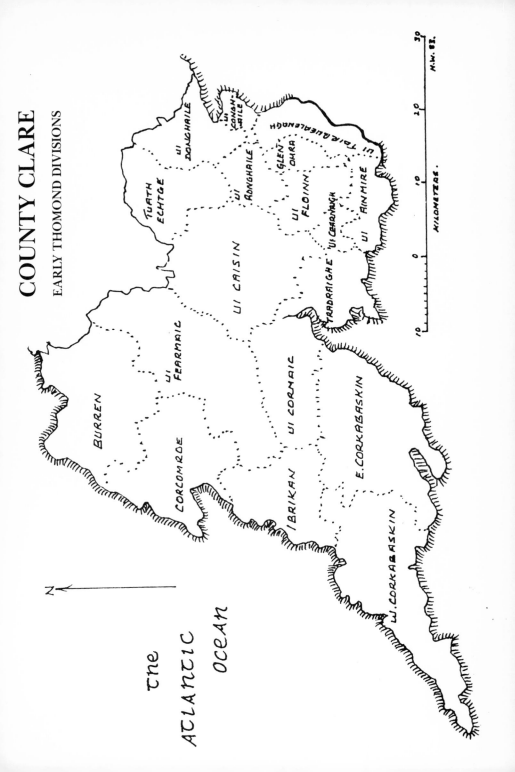

COUNTY CLARE
EARLY THOMOND DIVISIONS

THE ATLANTIC OCEAN

N

BURREN

CORCOMROE

UI FEARMAIC

TUATH ECHTGE

UI DONGHAILE

UI CONAN-MHAILE

UI RONGHAILE

GLENT OMRA

UI FLOINN

UI TAIRCHEACLAUGH

UI AINMIRE

UI CEARNACH

TRADRAIGHE

UI CAISIN

UI CORMAIC

I BRIKAN

E.CORKABASKIN

W.CORKABASKIN

KILOMETERS.

0        10        20        30

N.W. 83.

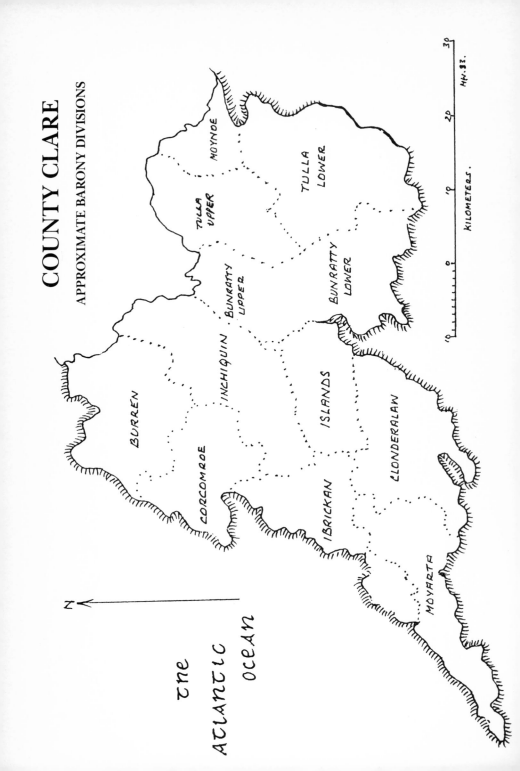

# COUNTY CLARE

## APPROXIMATE BARONY DIVISIONS

The ATLANTIC OCEAN

N

KILOMETERS.

MOYNOE

TULLA UPPER

TULLA LOWER

BUNRATTY UPPER

BUNRATTY LOWER

BURREN

INCHIQUIN

CORCOMROE

ISLANDS

IBRICKAN

CLONDERALAW

MOYARTA

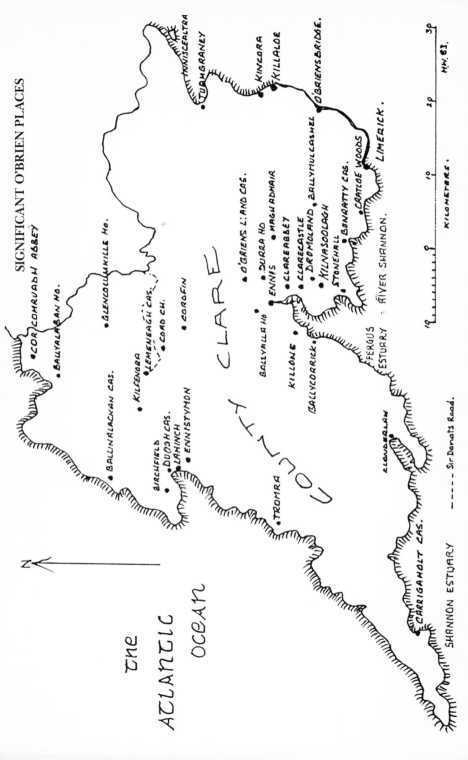

# COUNTY CLARE

## SIGNIFICANT O'BRIEN PLACES

THE ATLANTIC OCEAN

N

COUNTY CLARE

- CORCOMRUAGH ABBEY
- BALLYALABAN HO.
- BALLINALACKAN CAS.
- GLENCOLUMKILLE HO.
- KILFENORA
- LEMENEAGH CAS.
- COAD CH.
- COROFIN
- BIRCHFIELD
- DOUGH CAS.
- LAHINCH
- ENNISTYMON
- TROMRA
- O'BRIENS L: AND CAS.
- DURRA HO.
- ENNIS
- MAGH ADHAIR
- CLAREABBEY
- CLARECASTLE
- DROMOLAND
- BALLYMULCASHEL
- KILNASOOLAGH
- STONEHALL
- BUNRATTY CAS.
- CARTLOE WOODS
- LIMERICK.
- BALLYALLA HO
- KILLONE
- BALLYCORRICK.
- FERGUS ESTUARY
- RIVER SHANNON.
- CLOUGHOLAW
- CARRIGAHOLT CAS.
- SHANNON ESTUARY
- TUAMGRANEY
- INNISCEALTRA
- KINCORA
- KILLALOE
- O'BRIENSBRIDGE.

----- Sir Donats Road.

KILOMETERS.      H.W. 83.

# Some O'Brien Places

### Ara Castle, Co. Tipperary
This strong castle on the shore of Lough Derg, near Portroe, Co. Tipperary, was the home of a branch of the O'Briens descended from Brian Ruadh, forty-first King of Thomond, who was murdered by de Clare at Bunratty. It is now in ruins.

### Ballina Castle, Co. Tipperary
Nothing remains of this castle, which once stood on the site of the present creamery, just over the bridge from Killaloe. This plain fort of the O'Briens of Ara was standing at the end of the nineteenth century.

### Ballinalacken Castle, Co. Clare
This beautifully situated cliff-top tower house near Lisdoonvarna, and its nearby Georgian mansion, was the home of a branch descended from Donal Bacach O'Brien, who married Saibh O'Lochlin. 'Peter the Packer' (Lord O'Brien) lived here.

### Ballyalla, Co. Clare
This house and magnificent demesne, five kilometres north of Ennis, was the home of Mrs Vere O'Brien and her family in the early twentieth century. She founded the Clare Embroidery School here. A sanitorium was located near the present lakeside amenity area.

### Ballyallaban House, Co. Clare
A delightful house situated on a seven-hundred-acre demesne, Ballyallaban was for many years the property of a branch of the O'Briens. It is at the end of a long drive five kilometres south of Ballyvaughan.

### Ballycorrick Castle, Co. Clare
Situated 1.5 kilometres north of Ballynacally, Ballycorrick Castle and its plain two storey Georgian house is on land which was leased to Charles O'Brien in perpetuity from 1641. His family lived here for several generations.

### Ballyetragh Castle, Co. Waterford
Near the centre of the county is the castle settled by John O'Brien of Comeragh, after he escaped from Cromwell. His descendant, Pierse O'Brien, was living there in 1887.

### Barnakill Castle, Co. Waterford
This castle near Kilrossanty was built by the Waterford O'Briens, who had

resided in the area since 1413, when Turlough ('the Bald') O'Brien, deposed King of Thomond, settled here.

### Bealboru, Co. Clare

Probably situated at the highest point in the town of Killaloe, where the Roman Catholic church now stands, this royal palace of Brian Boru has completely disappeared. It commanded a magnificent view of the Shannon valley and Lough Derg.

### Birchfield, Co. Clare

Cornelius O'Brien, the well-known member of parliament, built this imposing castellated house in the early nineteenth century. The ruins are situated off the coast road 1.5 kilometres north-west of Liscannor. It was disused at the beginning of the twentieth century.

### Brooke Lodge, Co. Waterford

This originally Georgian house near Lemybrien was the property of Robert O'Brien, uncle of the Baronne de Goya Borras of Madrid, in the latter part of the nineteenth century. He was descended from a family settled in the area since 1413.

### Bunratty Castle, Co. Clare See page 14

### Cahermoyle, Co. Limerick See page 42

### Carrigaholt Castle, Co. Clare

This narrow tower house, which overlooks the harbour and the Shannon estuary from its cliff-top site, was the home of Sir Daniel O'Brien, who was created Viscount Clare in 1662, and of his descendants.

### Carrigogonnell Castle, Co. Limerick See page 16

### Cashel Rock, Co. Tipperary See page 12

### Castletown House, Co. Fermanagh See page 38

### Clare Abbey, Co. Clare

The fine ruined abbey behind the village of Clarecastle was founded by Donal Mór O'Brien in 1195 for the Canons Regular of St Augustine. It is now in the hands of the Board of Works.

### Clarecastle, Co. Clare

The remains of a circular tower still stand overlooking the river Fergus. Nineteenth-century barrack buildings were built in the extensive bawn of this O'Brien fortress, which was for a time the county's capital.

### Cliveden, Buckinghamshire, England

This magnificent Thames-side estate and its eighteenth-century house became the property of the Earl of Inchiquin through his marriage to the Countess of Orkney. The house, which was burnt down in 1795 and later rebuilt, became the property of Lord Astor in the twentieth century. Some of the original pavilions and garden layout remain. It is now an hotel.

### Clonroad Castle, Co. Clare
Now completely demolished, this extensive thirteenth-century castle, close to the town of Ennis, was the headquarters of the Earls of Thomond. In 1712, the eighth Earl of Thomond leased the property to Francis Gore.

### Clontarf, Co. Dublin
North of the capital city is the site of the famous battle fought in 1014, when Brian Boru, High King of Ireland, was slaughtered as he defeated the Danes.

### Coad Church, Co. Clare
Close by the Corofin to Kilfenora road, Coad church was reputedly built by Máire Ruadh. Certainly her daughters, Honora and Mary, were buried there. Some say she too was interred in this simple building situated on a slight rise overlooking Lough Inchiquin.

### Comeragh Castle, Co. Waterford
Near the source of the river Tay in the Comeragh mountains is the fifteenth-century castle where a branch of the family lived until the late seventeenth century. Little now remains, only rubble in an emerald green field reputedly fertilised through the burial of the family's slain enemies. Four sons of Derby O'Brien were hanged here after the castle was taken by Cromwell. John, the fifth son, escaped to Helvick Head.

### Corcumruadh Abbey, Co. Clare
This beautifully situated abbey near Ballyvaughan, also known as 'the abbey of the fertile rock', was built in 1194 by Donal O'Brien, King of Thomond, or by his son, Donough Cairbreagh, six years later. Dedicated to the Virgin Mary, it contains the effigy of the slain Conor O'Brien.

### Coronation Stone, Co. Tipperary
On the summit of the Rock of Cashel, near the main entrance door, is the carved coronation stone of the Kings of Munster. Here they were crowned and received tribute. It is surmounted by an early cross depicting a clothed figure of Christ on one side, and a bishop on the other.

### Cratloe Woods, Co. Clare
A long, two storey, thirteen bay, gable-ended house, having a central one

bay breakfront, and tall Elizabethan-style chimney stacks. The original eighteenth-century house was extended and renovated in 1840. The Stafford O'Briens moved here from Stonehall. Surrounded by an eleven-hundred-acre estate in 1878, the house is now the residence of Robert Guy Stafford O'Brien, and his cousins, the Brickendens. It is close to Limerick.

### Devenish Church, Co. Fermanagh
Built in 1890, this delightful church at Monea contains a window from the nearby Devenish Island abbey, a copy of which was presented to Knock, Co. Mayo. It was dedicated to St Molaise in memory of John Dawson Brien, D.L., of Castletown.

### Dough Castle, Co. Clare
This O'Connor castle soon fell into O'Brien hands. By the south of the Ennistymon river, it remained in the hands of the Ennistymon O'Briens until they moved to their new house at the beginning of the eighteenth century.

### Dromoland Castle, Co. Clare See page 32

### Durra House, Co. Clare
Now an impressive ruin, this large house was, in 1887, the home of Pierce O'Brien, J.P. His daughter, Catherine Amelia, the accomplished mosaic artist, was a founder member of 'The Tower of Glass'– the stained glass co-operative studio. Her work can be seen in Ennis Church of Ireland.

### Ennis Abbey, Co. Clare
Built circa 1240 by Donough Cairbreach O'Brien for the conventual Franciscan friars, this abbey contains many family tombs, including those of Turlough, King of Thomond (d. 1306), Dermot, Prince of Thomond (1313), Mahon, King of Thomond (1370), and some of the Earls. It is maintained by the Board of Works.

### Ennistymon House, Co. Clare
Now the Falls Hotel, this delightful house overlooking the Ennistymon Falls became the home of a branch founded by Sir Donald O'Brien, Knight, of nearby Dough, who died in 1579. It later became the property of the Macnamaras.

### Glencolumkille House, Co. Clare
In 1837, Terence O'Brien owned this small Georgian, two storey house, which faces down the glen towards Boston. The family ran the nearby racecourse.

**Holy Cross Abbey, Co. Tipperary**
On the right bank of the river Suir, this Cistercian foundation has been recently restored as the parish church. It was built by Donal Mór O'Brien in the twelfth century as a sanctuary for a fragment of the Holy Cross which Pope Pascal II gave the King's grandfather, Murtagh, in 1110.

**Inchiquin Castle, Co. Clare**
This interesting castle stands on the shore of Lough Inchiquin, near Corofin. It was the home of Murrough, Baron Inchiquin and first Earl of Thomond, who died in 1581. The castle is now in ruins.

**Inniscealtra, Co. Clare**
An island on Lough Derg off Mountshannon, which is also known as Holy Island, Inniscealtra contains the ruins of a monastic foundation of the O'Briens. Here also is a monument to Sir Turlough O'Brien, Baronet, of Ara, and his wife, who died in 1626 and 1628 respectively.

**Jockey Hall, Co. Kildare** See page 34

**Kilcor, Co. Cork**
Near Rathcormack, where there is a family vault, are Kilcor and Pellick castles, about four kilometres apart. Here were the homes of a family descended from the O'Briens of Ara. They inherited Kilcor through marriage to the Barrys, and Pellick by purchase from Lord Buttevant in 1613.

**Kildare Street, Dublin**
Number two, which later became part of the Kildare Street Club, was a town house of the Earls of Inchiquin. It was built to the design of Edward Nicholson. The fourth Earl of Inchiquin died in 1777, but his widow was living there in 1784.

**Killaloe Cathedral, Co. Clare**
This delightfully simple cruciform church, with its tall, narrow tripartite window, was founded by Donal Mór O'Brien in the twelfth century. Several O'Briens were bishops of the diocese.

**Killone, Co. Clare**
The pleasantly situated lakeside abbey and the demesne surrounding it were sold by Edward O'Brien, who lived in the house above (now called New Hall, and added to), to his nephew, Charles MacDonnell, in 1764. The Augustinian abbey was founded by Donal Mór O'Brien in 1190.

**Killone, Co. Clare**
The pleasantly situated lakeside abbey and the demesne surrounding it

were sold by Edward O'Brien, who lived in the house above (now called New Hall, and added to), to his nephew, Charles MacDonnell, in 1764. The Augustinian abbey was founded by Donal Mór O'Brien in 1190.

### Kilnasoolagh Church, Co. Clare

This delightful Gothic-revival church, which was reconstructed by the Pain brothers in the early nineteenth century on an ancient site, contains a magnificent monument to Sir Donough O'Brien, first Baronet, who moved to Dromoland from Lemeneagh in about 1685. There are also later memorials to his branch of the family. In the graveyard is the vault of the Lords Inchiquin.

### Kincora, Co. Clare

Ceanncora (the head of the weir) which is situated about two kilometres from Killaloe, is today a tree-covered mound on an eminence overlooking what was a ford, before it was deepened during the construction of the Shannon hydro-electric scheme in 1926. It was a major palace of Brian Boru. Teige, King of Munster, died here in 1086.

### Lemeneagh Castle, Co. Clare See page 24

### Limerick Cathedral, Limerick See page 20

### Lohort Castle, Co. Cork

Although originally a MacCarthy castle, this fifteenth-century tower house became the home of Sir Timothy O'Brien, Baronet, and his family in the nineteenth century. It has rounded corners and is surrounded by geometrically-arranged landscape gardens. There is a fine nineteenth-century castellated gatehouse.

### Magh Adhair, Co. Clare

Situated a short distance from Quin, Magh Adhair, with its man-made mound in the centre of a natural amphitheatre, was the traditional inauguration place of the O'Briens as Kings of Thomond.

### Moor Park, Shropshire, England

Although in 1861 considered as a possible British royal residence, but turned down in favour of Sandringham, which was nearer London, this basically Queen Anne house became the property of the fifteenth Baron Inchiquin through marriage in 1896 with the daughter of Johnston Jonas Foster, who had bought it in 1873.

### O'Brien's Bridge, Co. Clare

This picturesque village, with its ancient bridge crossing the river Shannon, was the site of Murrough O'Brien's (d. 1581) castle. First Earl of Thomond and Baron Inchiquin, he also lived at Inchiquin Castle. Nothing now remains of his O'Briensbridge fortress, but the bridge was probably built by him.

### Ratisbon, Germany
Now known as Regensburg, this German town is the site of the abbey of St Peter, which was founded and endowed by Conor na Catharach O'Brien, who was proclaimed King of Munster in 1120, and was generally acknowledged King of Ireland.

### Rostellan, Co. Cork See page 28

### St Columba's College, Co. Dublin
This well-known public school at Rathfarnham, south of Dublin, was founded in 1841. The O'Briens were instrumental in its foundation, and many members of the family were students there. Amongst the first managers was Augustus O'Brien of Stonehall.

### Salterbridge, Co. Waterford
Halfway between Cappaquin and Lismore, this demesne and castle once belonged to the O'Briens of Comeragh. A mid-nineteenth-century, five bay house facing the river Blackwater has been added to the original.

### Stonehall, Co. Clare
Little now remains of the substantial house of Henry O'Brien, son of Sir Donough O'Brien, first Baronet, who married Suzannah Stafford, daughter of Lord Carbery. His descendants later moved to Cratloe Woods.

### Tara, Co. Meath
Here are the huge earthworks, now labelled by the Irish government, which show the extent of the royal palace and outworks of the High Kings of Ireland, such as Brian Boru. It overlooks the wide plain of Meath.

### Trinity College, Dublin
Dublin University has been the Alma Mater of many O'Briens, including Donough MacConor O'Brien (1614), the fifth Earl of Thomond (1613), and Sir Lucius O'Brien, third Baronet (1748). It was founded in the reign of Queen Elizabeth I. Brian Boru's harp is preserved here.

### Tromroe Castle, Co. Clare
An O'Brien castle still stands on this bleak site overlooking the Atlantic. Here, in 1280, Dermot Mór O'Brien received the annual gift of twelve tuns of wine for protecting Galway from pirates. He also used his castle on Innisheer, the smallest of the Aran Islands, to benefit the Galway merchants in their trade.

## Tuamgraney Church, Co. Clare

Reputedly the oldest of Ireland's churches to be in continuous use, this tenth-century foundation was restored by Brian Boru, who worshipped here before commencing his journey to Clontarf to do battle with the Danes. It was restored in the nineteenth century.

Killaloe, Co. Clare, from an old print

# Major late 19th century O'Brien landowners

BRIEN, The Misses and others, Newcastle House, Greystairs: 1,843 acres in Co. Leitrim

BRIEN, John D., Castletown, Monea, Enniskillen: 5,085 acres in Co. Fermanagh

BRYAN, George Leopold, M.P., Jenkinstown, Kilkenny: 1,627 acres in Co. Kildare; 8,209 acres in Co. Kilkenny; 3,055 acres in Co. Meath

BRYAN, John Hamilton, J.P., Prospect Hill, Dunmanway: 683 acres in Co. Cork

BRYAN, Loftus Anthony, Bormount, Enniscorthy: 6,135 acres in Co. Wexford

BRYAN, Thomas, Gurteen, Galway: 609 acres in Co. Tipperary

BRYAN, Reverend William Butler, A.M., Woodenbridge, Avoca, Co. Wicklow: 782 acres in Co. Kilkenny

INCHIQUIN, Lord, Edward Donough O'Brien, fourteenth Baron, J.P., D.L., V.L., Dromoland, Newmarket-on-Fergus; Hereford House, Park Street, London W: 20,321 acres in Co. Clare

O'BRIEN, Denis Bray, J.P., Ardfert House, Thurles: 1,029 acres in Co. Tipperary

O'BRIEN, Denis, Carlow: 2,448 acres in Co. Tipperary

O'BRIEN, Denis, Dalkey: 933 acres in Co. Cork

O'BRIEN, Edward William, B.A., J.P., D.L., Cahermoyle, Newcastle: 4,990 acres in Co. Limerick

O'BRIEN, Henry, Reps. of, Queenstown: 505 acres in Co. Cork

O'BRIEN, Horace Stafford, J.P., Cratloe Woods, Cratloe: 655 acres in Co. Clare

O'BRIEN, James, J.P., D.L., Ballinalacken, Lisdoonvarna: 5,575 acres in Co. Clare; 36 acres in Co. Limerick

O'BRIEN, John Stackpoole, J.P., Parkview, Tanderagee, Co. Armagh: 1,769 acres in Co. Clare

O'BRIEN, John, Cork: 748 acres in Co. Kerry

O'BRIEN, John, Reps. of: 3,688 acres in King's County

O'BRIEN, Captain Michael, Rockfield, Kilpeacon, Co. Limerick: 77 acres in Co. Limerick; 619 acres in Co. Tipperary

O'BRIEN, Michael, Assolas, Kanturk: 793 acres in counties Cork and Limerick

O'BRIEN, Mrs Annie Donata, 31 Queen's Road, Everton, Liverpool: 664 acres in Co. Tipperary

O'BRIEN, Mrs Jane, Waterloo Road, Dublin: 547 acres in Co. Leitrim

O'BRIEN, Mrs Mary, England: 805 acres in Co. Tipperary

O'BRIEN, Sir Patrick, J.P., D.L., M.P., Borris-in-Ossory, Queen's County; 21 Bryanston Square, London W: 146 acres in King's County; 824 acres in Queen's County

O'BRIEN, Robert Francis, J.P., Killeshandra: 1,091 acres in Co. Cavan

O'BRIEN, Robert                                           )
O'BRIEN, Mrs Margaret, Goothill, Mohill ) 1,014 acres in Co. Longford
DUNDAS, H., Lismoy, Newtownforbes      )

O'BRIEN, Timothy, Ailesbury House, Merrion, Co. Dublin: 22 acres in Co. Dublin; 759 acres in Co. Tipperary

O'BRIEN, Timothy, Limerick: 1,018 acres in Limerick

O'BRIEN, Captain William Acheson, J.P., Drumsilla, Carrigallan: 1,489 acres in Co. Leitrim

O'BRIEN, William, Riversdale, Ruskey, Co. Roscommon: 677 acres in Co. Leitrim

## Distribution summary of 19th century O'Brien lands

| | | | |
|---|---|---|---|
| Co. Cavan | 1,091 | Co. Leitrim | 4,556 |
| Co. Clare | 28,320 | Co. Limerick | 6,728 |
| Co. Cork | 2,307 | Co. Longford | 1,014* |
| Co. Fermanagh | 5,085 | Co. Meath | 3,055 |
| Co. Kerry | 748 | Co. Offaly (Queen's County) | 824 |
| Co. Kildare | 1,627 | Co. Tipperary | 6,930 |
| Co. Kilkenny | 9,773 | Co. Wexford | 6,135 |
| Co. Laois (King's County) | 3,834 | | |

Total acres owned in Ireland: 82,049


O'BRIEN, Horace Stafford, Blatherwycke Park, etc: 562 acres in Rutlandshire; 1,955 acres in Northamptonshire

Total acres owned in England: 2,517


* Two-thirds share with H. Dundas

# A Short List of O'Brien Biography

BRIAN Boru See page 10

BRIEN, Alan. Journalist and film critic, columnist and broadcaster. b. early twentieth century.

BRIEN, Andrew. Commander, R.N. Son of John Brien of Monea. b. 1784 (Stralongford), d. early nineteenth century.

BRIEN, John, D.L., J.P. Captain, Tyrone Militia; High Sheriff, Co. Fermanagh. b. 1776, d. 1856 (Co. Fermanagh).

BRIEN, Lowther. Crown Solicitor of Co. Fermanagh. b. 1774 (Co. Cavan), d. 1841 (Co. Fermanagh).

OBERON, Merle. Stage name of film actress Estelle Merle O'Brien Thompson. b. early twentieth century (Tasmania).

O'BREEN, Adriaan Johan. Alderman of Rotterdam. Captain in Dutch army. b. eighteenth century (Rotterdam).

O'BREEN, Gerrit. Governor, Netherlands Trading Company, Amsterdam. b. 1804 (Holland), d. 1880.

O'BREEN, Herman. Lawyer and notary of Leyden. b. 1810 (Holland), d. 1880 (Holland).

O'BRIAIN, Barra. Hon. President of the Irish Circuit Court, ex officio High Court. Writer. b. twentieth century (Dublin).

O'BRIAIN, Ceallach. Priest, OFM, theologian (D.D.), Franciscan Provincial, philosopher. b. early twentieth century (Limerick).

O'BRIAIN, Conchubhar. Priest, theologian (D.D.) and poet. b. 1650 (Ireland), d. 1720 (Ireland).

O'BRIAIN, Liam. Republican. Linguist (Professor of Romance Languages, UCD), politician, author. b. 1880 (Dublin), d. 1974 (Dublin).

O'BRIEN, Andrew J. National teacher, Senator (Fine Gael), vice-president G.A.A. b. early twentieth century (Co. Cavan).

O'BRIEN, Anna Maria Sydney. Married Archdeacon Spooner (spoonerisms). Daughter of Sir Lucius O'Brien, third Baronet. b. 1784, d. 1846 (England).

O'BRIEN, Anne, Lady Inchiquin. Wife of sixteenth Baron, daughter of Viscount Chelmsford, Viceroy of India. b. 1898 (Dorset), d. 1973 (Co. Clare).

O'BRIEN, Anthony. Chevalier of the Royal Cambodian Order. Engineer. Director General, Shell Oil, Cambodia. b. early twentieth century (Dublin).

O'BRIEN, Antoinette Charlotte. Daughter of Charles, Marshal Thomond. Married le Duc de Choiseul-Praslin. b. circa 1759, d. 1808 (France)

O'BRIEN, Arthur Henry. Lawyer and onetime militiaman. b. 1865 (Canada), d. twentieth century.

O'BRIEN,, Aubrey John. Deputy Commissioner of the Punjab. Author. b. 1870 (England), d. twentieth century.

O'BRIEN, Attie (Frances Marcella). Poetess and authoress. b. 1840 (Ennis) d. 1883.

O'BRIEN, Augustus. First co-Manager of St Columba's College, Rathfarnham. b. 1811, d. 1857 (Ireland).

O'BRIEN, Brendan Edward. Physician, Meath Hospital, Dublin, 1943-75. Board member of I.A.W.S. and Smyly's Homes. Lecturer T.C.D. Son of W. Dermod O'Brien. b. 1903 (Co. Limerick), d. 1984.

O'BRIEN, Brendan Patrick. Musician (RTE Orchestra, Royal Philharmonic Orchestra, etc.). b. twentieth century (Dublin).

O'BRIEN, Brian. Order of Orange Nassau (1952). Solicitor and legal adviser to British Ministries of Health, Housing and Local Government. b. twentieth century (South Africa).

O'BRIEN, Palliser Teige. C.S.I., O.B.E., M.C. Brigadier. Director of Intelligence (India Command). Durra family. b. late nineteenth century (Co. Clare), d. twentieth century.

O'BRIEN, Bryan Justin. C.M.G. Chief Secretary, North Borneo, etc. Joint editor, *Handbook of Cyprus*. b. early twentieth century (England).

O'BRIEN, Charles, fifth Viscount Clare. Served James II at Limerick, etc. Commanded three Franco-Irish regiments. b. seventeenth century (Co. Clare), d. 1706 (Ramillies).

O'BRIEN, Charles, sixth Viscount Clare. Marshal of France (1757). C-in-C of Languedoc. b. 1699 (France), d. 1761 (Montpellier).

O'BRIEN, Charles, seventh (and last) Viscount Clare. Colonel, Regiment of Clare. b. early eighteenth century, d. 1774 (Paris).

O'BRIEN, Charles M. President, Institute of Actuaries (1976-78); Governor, Westminster School. b. early twentieth century (England).

O'BRIEN, Charles Richard. Lt. Colonel. Governor and C-in-C, Seychelles. b. 1859 (India), d. twentieth century.

O'BRIEN, Charlotte Grace. See page 44.

O'BRIEN, Christopher. Created Baron Inchiquin at Kilkenny. Besieged Ballyalla Castle 1641. d. circa 1665.

O'BRIEN, Christopher Michael. Physician and author. b. 1861 (Co. Roscommon), d. twentieth century.

O'BRIEN, Conor. Eighteenth Baron Inchiquin. Only son of Hon. Fionn O'Brien. Businessman. Married Helen O'Farrell 1988. b. 1943 (England).

O'BRIEN, Conor. Barrister and Editor (*Evening Press, Sunday Independent*). b. twentieth century (Dublin).

O'BRIEN, Conor Cruise. Author, diplomat, politician, Senator. Pro-Chancellor, T.C.D. b. twentieth century (Dublin).

O'BRIEN, Constantine. Bishop of Killaloe. Succeeded Donat O'Brien 1179 after ten years' vacancy. d. 1194 (Co. Clare).

O'BRIEN, Cornelius. M.P. for Co. Clare. Lived Liscannor. b. eighteenth century, d. 1857 (Co. Clare).

O'BRIEN, Daniel. Progenitor of the Dutch O'Breens. Married Helena Barry (1618) at Emmerick. Carrigogonnell family. b. sixteenth century, d. seventeenth century.

O'BRIEN, Daniel. First Viscount Clare. Ardent Catholic militant and M.P. b. circa 1580 (Co. Clare), d. 1663 (Co. Clare).

O'BRIEN, David E. Sixth Baronet. b. 1902 (London), d. 1982 (Co. Tipperary).

O'BRIEN, The Hon. Deirdre J. F. Eldest daughter of sixteenth Baron Inchiquin. Married Dr H. Beecher Chapin of New York. b. twentieth century.

O'BRIEN, (William) Dermod. Artist. President R.H.S. (1910-45). D.L. Grandson of William Smith O'Brien. b. 1865 (Co. Limerick), d. 1945 (Dublin).

O'BRIEN, Dermot Patrick. Q.C. Crown Court Recorder, Western Circuit (England). b. 1939.

O'BRIEN, Dillon. Poet and novelist. Wrote about American-Irish. b. 1824 (Co. Roscommon), d. 1882 (USA).

O'BRIEN, Sir Donald. Founder of Duagh or Ennistymon O'Briens, and Governor of Co. Clare (1576). b. sixteenth century, d. 1579 (Co. Clare).

O'BRIEN, Donal Mór. King of Munster. Founded Limerick, Killaloe cathedrals; Holy Cross Abbey etc. b. twelfth century (Ireland), d. 1194 (Ireland).

O'BRIEN, Donat Henchy. Admiral, R.N. b. circa 1785 (Co. Clare), d. 1857.

O'BRIEN, Donough. Son of Brian Boru. Joint King of Ireland (1014-23). Monk (1023-c.1064). b. Ireland, d.1064 (Rome).

O'BRIEN, Donough. Fourth Earl of Thomond. Lord President of Munster. b. sixteenth century, d. 1624.

O'BRIEN, Sir Donough. First Baronet of Lemeneagh and Dromoland (1686). See page 22.

O'BRIEN, The. Hon. Donough. Author of *History of the O'Briens from Brian Boru to 1945*. Barrister, genealogist. b. 1879, d. 1953 (Egypt).

O'BRIEN, Donough E. F. Sixteenth Baron Inchiquin. See page 46.

O'BRIEN, Edna. Authoress and scriptwriter. b. twentieth century (Co. Clare).

O'BRIEN, Sir Edward. Second Baronet of Dromoland. M.P. (Peterborough and Clare) 1727-65. b. 1705 (Co. Clare), d. 1765.

O'BRIEN, Edward. Fourth Baronet. M.P. (Ennis and Clare) (1795-1826) b. 1773 (Co. Clare), d. 1837.

O'BRIEN, Edward. Author. b. 1808 (Co. Clare), d. 1837.

O'BRIEN, Edward. C.B.E. Lieut. Colonel, Indian Army. Irish forty-metres hurdles champion. b. 1872 (India), d. twentieth century.

O'BRIEN, Edward. Captain, R.N. Was blown up on the *Dartmouth*, but survived. b. 1735 (Co. Louth), d. 1801 (Co. Cork).

O'BRIEN, Edward. Deputy Commissioner, Punjab. b. 1843, d. 1894.

O'BRIEN, Edward Conor M. Author, yachtsman. Sailed round the world in *Saoirse* (1923-25), (and was first to display the tri-colour internationally), and to Falkland Islands (1927). Mountaineer. Irish speaker and Sinn Fein member. b. 1880 (Ireland), d. twentieth century.

O'BRIEN, Edward Donough. Fourteenth Baron. See page 36.

O'BRIEN, Edward George. R.N. (Ret. 1830). Founder of Canadian family branch. J.P. and Colonel of Militia. b. 1799, d. 1875 (Canada).

O'BRIEN, Edward Henry. Surgeon R.N. (Copenhagen etc.) b. 1772 (Cavan), d. 1859 (Co. Donegal).

O'BRIEN, Edmond. American actor, *The Barefoot Contessa* etc. b. early twentieth century (New York).

O'BRIEN, Edmund Donough John. C.B. Brigadier General. Served in South Africa etc. b. 1858 (India), d. twentieth century.

O'BRIEN, Ellen Lucy (Nelly). Eldest daughter of Edward William O'Brien. Gaelic Leaguer. Painter and miniaturist. A founder of Carrigaholt Irish Language College. b. 1864 (Co. Limerick), d. 1925 (Ireland).

O'BRIEN, Ernest Edward. Editor, *Halifax Guardian*. b.1869, d. twentieth century.

O'BRIEN, Most Reverend Eris M. Roman Catholic Archbishop of Canberra-Goulburn. Author. b. late nineteenth century (Australia).

O'BRIEN, Evelene. Medical doctor. Governor, Dundrum Mental Hospital. Writer. b. early twentieth century (Co. Sligo).

O'BRIEN. Fergus. Fine Gael Solicitor. T.D. Onetime Lord Mayor of Dublin. b. twentieth century (Dublin).

O'BRIEN. Fionnula. Daughter of King Conor Mór O'Brien. Married Hugh Roe O'Donnell. b. fifteenth century, d. sixteenth century.

O'BRIEN, FitzJames. Playwright and short story writer. b. 1828 (Co. Limerick), d. 1862 (USA).

O'BRIEN, Flann. Pen name of humourist author Brian O Nuallain. b. 1912 (Strabane), d. 1966 (Dublin).

O'BRIEN, Florence Darby. Captain, Regiment of Clare. Knight of St Louis. d. 1743 (Landrecies), d. circa 1785.

O'BRIEN, Frank. Professor, English Literature, Virginia. b. twentieth century (New York).

O'BRIEN, Sir Frederick Lucius. First Chairman, N. Ireland Housing Trust. Philanthropist. b. late nineteenth century.

O'BRIEN, Sir Frederick William FitzGerald. K.B., Q.C. Lawyer, Sheriff-Principal. b. 1917 (Scotland).

O'BRIEN, George A.T. Senator, Economist (Professor UCD 1926-61). Author. b. 1892 (Dublin), d. 1973 (Dublin).

O'BRIEN, Geraldine Mary. Landscape and flower artist. Married d. Hely Hutchinson. b. twentieth century (Limerick).

O'BRIEN, Gerard W. Chartered accountant. Emeritus Professor, UCD. b. twentieth century (Dublin).

O'BRIEN, The Hon. Grania Rachel. Younger daughter of sixteenth Baron Inchiquin. Social Secretary (Diplomatic). Married Hugh W. L. Weir. b. twentieth century (London).

O'BRIEN, Henry. Antiquary and author (*Round Towers of Ireland*, 1839). b. 1808 (Co. Kerry), d. 1835 (Middlesex).

O'BRIEN, Henry. K.C. Barrister. Editor, *Toronto Law Journal*. Oarsman, author. b. 1836 (Ontario), d. twentieth century.

O'BRIEN, The Hon. Henry Barnaby. M.C., D.L. Lieut. Colonel, Irish Guards. Wounded. Mentioned in dispatches. b. 1887 (Co. Clare), d. circa 1976 (Scotland).

O'BRIEN, Honora. Daughter of Conor O'Brien of Lemeneagh. Married Donough O'Brien of Dough. b. circa 1635 (Co. Clare), d. circa 1710.

O'BRIEN, Hugh. American T.V. actor (*The Legend of Wyatt Earp*). b. twentieth century (Rochester, NY).

O'BRIEN, Rt. Hon. Ignatius J. Baron Shannon of Cork. Attorney General for Ireland (1912). Barrister. b. 1857 (Cork), d. twentieth century.

O'BRIEN, James. Third Marquess of Thomond. Admiral of the White, G.C.H. b. 1769, d. 1855.

O'BRIEN. James 'Bronterre'. Chartist and lecturer. b. 1805 (Co. Longford), d. 1864 (London).

O'BRIEN, James George. Landscape artist (as O'Brien & Oben). b. circa 1758, d. circa 1820.

O'BRIEN, Right Reverend Monsignor James J. D.D. Theologian. Domestic Prelate to Pope Leo XIII. Rector, University of New South Wales.

O'BRIEN, James J. Army Colonel. b. nineteenth century (Co. Clare), d. nineteenth century.

O'BRIEN, Right Reverend James I. Bishop of Ossory (Church of Ireland). Author. b. 1792 (Co. Wexford), d. 1874 (London).

O'BRIEN, Jeremiah. American seaman. Captured *Diligence* and other British vessels. b. circa 1740 (Co. Cork), d. 1818 (USA).

O'BRIEN, John W. Rector and Vice-Chancellor, Concordia University. Economist, author. b. twentieth century (Canada).

O'BRIEN, Kate. Travel writer and biographer. b. 1897 (Limerick), d. circa 1974 (Canterbury).

O'BRIEN, Ken. Younger son of Horace Donough O'Brien, FRCSI, FRACS, OA. Chief sailmaker for yacht *Australia II* (Americas Cup 1983). b. Australia.

O'BRIEN, Pamela Katherine Wilmer (Kitty). Artist. President of Irish Watercolour Society. R.H.A. Married Dr Brendan O'Brien. b. early twentieth century, d. 1982 (Dublin).

O'BRIEN, Lawrence. American Democratic politician. Senator (1952). U.S. Postmaster General. b. early twentieth century (Massachusetts).

O'BRIEN, Leslie K. Baron O'Brien of Lothbury (1973). P.C., C.B.E. President, British Bankers' Association. Governor, Bank of England. b. 1908 (London).

O'BRIEN, Lucius. M.P. for Clare (1703-14). Married Catherine Keightly. b. 1675 (Co. Clare), d. 1717 (Paris).

O'BRIEN, Very Reverend Lucius H. Dean of Limerick (Church of Ireland). Theologian, illustrator. Second son of William S. O'Brien. b. 1842, d. 1913.

O'BRIEN, Sir Lucius Henry. Third Baronet. See page 30.

O'BRIEN, Lucius James. Professor of Medical Jurisprudence, Toronto University. b. 1796 (England), d. 1879 (Canada).

O'BRIEN, Lucius Richard. Landscape artist. First President, Royal Canadian Academy. b. 1832 (Canada), d. 1899 (Canada).

O'BRIEN, Lucius William. Fifteenth Baron Inchiquin, M.P., D.L., H.S. and J.P. Member of Irish Senate, 1921. b. 1864, d. 1929 (Co. Clare).

O'BRIEN, Luke. Vice-President, Municipal Authorities of Ireland. Politician. b. early twentieth century (Co. Galway).

O'BRIEN, Máire Ruadh. See page 18.

O'BRIEN, Margaret. Teacher, novelist, land and seascape artist. b. early twentieth century (Cork).

O'BRIEN, Margaret (Angela M.). American actress and film star (*Little Women* etc.). b. twentieth century (California).

O'BRIEN, Matthew. Mathematician. b. 1814 (Co. Clare), d. 1855.

O'BRIEN, Maurice. The name of three Bishops of Kilfenora. One confirmed by Edward I in 1303 served twenty years. Another (nobleman) appointed 1491, d. 1510; and Maurice (Murtagh) (1491-1523).

O'BRIEN, Maurice. Appointed Bishop of Killaloe 1570; a minor 1576 (consecrated) to 1612.

O'BRIEN, Michael. 'Manchester Martyr'. Also known as William Gould. U.S. citizen. b. circa 1840 (Cork), d. 1867 (Manchester).

O'BRIEN, Right Reverend Monsignor Michael Joseph. Principal R.C. Chaplain, R.A.F. b. early twentieth century (Co. Waterford).

O'BRIEN, Michael. Commodore, R.N. with NATO H.Q. in Brussels. b. twentieth century.

O'BRIEN, Michael. M.D. of O'Brien's Rent a Car/Rent a Van, Cork. b. twentieth century.

O'BRIEN, Dr Michael Vincent. LL.D. Leading horsetrainer and sportsman. b. 1917 (Cashel).

O'BRIEN, Murrough. 'The Tanaiste'. Fifty-seventh King of Thomond (1540) and first Earl; first Baron Inchiquin. b. late fifteenth or early sixteenth century, d. 1551.

O'BRIEN, Murrough 'of the Burnings'. Soldier. Governor of Catalonia and Majorca. First Earl of Inchiquin. b. 1614 (Co. Clare), d. 1674 (Co. Cork).

O'BRIEN, Murrough. First Marquess of Thomond; fifth Earl of Inchiquin. b. 1726, d. 1808.

O'BRIEN, The Hon. Murrough. D.S.O., M.V.O. Aide-de-camp to Lord Lieutenant of Ireland. b. 1866 (Co. Clare), d. 1934.

O'BRIEN, Murrough Vere. Geologist, Director, Irish Geological Survey (1952-64). b. 1919 (Parteen, Co. Clare).

O'BRIEN, Oswald. FBIM. British Labour M.P. for Darlington (1983). b. 1928.

O'BRIEN, Owen. Printer. Trade Unionist. b. twentieth century (London).

O'BRIEN, Patrick. M.P. for N. Monaghan 1886, and for Kilkenny 1895. b. eighteenth century (Co. Offaly).

O'BRIEN, Patrick. Adoptive name of descendant of Brian Boru, Patrick Cotter, the 2.59 metres tall giant. b. 1760 (Co. Cork), d. 1806 (Bristol).

O'BRIEN, Patrick. American film actor (*The Last Hurrah* etc.) b. late nineteenth century (Milwaukee).

O'BRIEN, Paul (An tAth Paul O Briain). Priest and scholar of Irish. Author. Grand-nephew of Carolan. b. 1750 (Co. Meath), d. 1820 (Kildare).

O'BRIEN, Peter 'the Packer'. P.C., LL.D. Lord Chief Justice of Ireland. Baronet 1891; Baron 1900. b. 1842 (Co. Clare), d. 1914 (Co. Dublin).

O'BRIEN, Phaedrig. Seventeenth Baron Inchiquin. Geologist. b. 1900, d. 1982 (Co. Clare).

O'BRIEN, Raymond Francis. Chief Executive, Merseyside County Council. b. twentieth century (England).

O'BRIEN, Sir Richard. D.S.O., M.C. Chairman, British Manpower Services Commission. b. 1920 (London).

O'BRIEN, Robert. Uncle of the Spanish Baronne de Goya Borras. He was reputedly the last of the Brooke Lodge, Co. Waterford, family. b. early nineteenth century (Co. Waterford), d. circa 1887 (Co. Waterford).

O'BRIEN, Terence. The name of three Bishops of Killaloe, 1441, 1483 and 1546.

O'BRIEN, Right Reverend Terence Albert. Bishop of Emly. Theologian. b. 1600 (Co. Limerick), d. 1651 (Ireland).

O'BRIEN, Terence John. Diplomat. British Ambassador to Burma 1974. b. twentieth century (England).

O'BRIEN, Sir Timothy. First Baronet of Borris-in-Ossory, Lord Mayor of Dublin 1844, 1849. M.P. b. 1787, d. 1862 (Dublin).

O'BRIEN, Timothy. Civil servant. Secretary, Department of Lands. Author. b. twentieth century (Co. Kerry).

O'BRIEN, Timothy Brian. Designer. E.B.C. Chairman, British Theatre Designers. b. 1929.

O'BRIEN, Sir Timothy Carew. Third Baronet. J.P., D.L. Cricketer. Soldier. b. 1861 (Co. Cork), d. 1948.

O'BRIEN, Sir Thomas. Knight 1956. Labour M.P. Trade Unionist. Director, *Daily Herald*. b. early twentieth century.

O'BRIEN, Turlough. King of Ireland 1064. Received homage from Ulster. b. eleventh century, d. 1086 (Co. Clare).

O'BRIEN, Turlough ('the Bald'). Ancestor of Waterford O'Briens. Deposed 1370. b. fourteenth century, d. 1399.

O'BRIEN, Turlough. Seneschal of Corcumruadh and Burren. Poet. b. sixteenth century, d. 1623 (Co. Clare).

O'BRIEN, Turlough Aubrey. C.B.E. President, Institute of Public Relations. b. 1907.

O'BRIEN, Vincent. See Michael Vincent O'Brien.

O'BRIEN, William. Second Earl of Inchiquin. Son of Murrough 'of the Burnings'. Governor of Jamaica. b. 1638, d. 1692.

O'BRIEN, William. Fourth Earl of Inchiquin. See page 26.

O'BRIEN, William. Actor. Wit and comedy writer. Receiver General for Dorset. b. circa 1738 (Co. Clare), d. circa 1815 (Dorset).

O'BRIEN, William. Judge, Irish Circuit. b. 1832 (Co. Cork), d. 1901 (Ireland).

O'BRIEN, William. Journalist, author. Nationalist. M.P. for Cork (1900). b. 1852 (Co. Cork), d. 1928 (Co. Cork).

O'BRIEN, William. Trade Unionist. President, I.T.U. Congress. b. 1881 (Co. Cork), d. 1968 (Co. Wicklow).

O'BRIEN, William. Businessman and Company Director. b. twentieth century (Co. Kerry).

O'BRIEN, William. J.P. British Labour M.P. for Normanton. b. twentieth century.

O'BRIEN, Sir William Donough. K.C.B., D.S.C. Admiral R.N. C-in-C, Western Fleet. b. 1916.

O'BRIEN, William Shoney. Millionaire. b. 1825 (Co. Offaly), d. 1878.

O'BRIEN, William Smith. See page 40.

O'BRIEN-BUTLER, Pierse E. Consul General, Yannan-fu, etc. (China). b. 1858 (Co. Clare), d. twentieth century.

O'BRIEN-MORAN, Edward J. Chairman, Dental Health Committee. Author. b. early twentieth century (Ireland).

O'BRIEN-TWOHIG, Joseph P. C.B.E., D.S.O. Brigadier. Barrister. Merchant. b. early twentieth century (Co. Cork).

O'BRIEN-TWOHIG, Michael J. O.B.E. Colonel. King's Messenger. b. late nineteenth century (Cornwall).

O'BRYAN, Hon. Sir Norman. Knight 1958. Judge, Australia (Victoria Supreme Court). Lecturer, Melbourne University. b. 1894 (Melbourne).

The eigtheenth Baron and Baroness Inchiquin
taken at Dromoland Castle before their wedding in 1988

# Some books relating to the O'Briens

Ainsworth, J.F. *The Inchiquin Manuscripts.* Irish Manuscript Commission, Dublin, 1960.

Burke, Sir Bernard. *Burke's Peerage* and *Burke's Landed Gentry of Ireland*, Burke's Peerage Ltd, London, 1912-1970.

Curley, Walter J. P. *Monarchs in Waiting*, Dodd, Mead & Co., New York, 1973.

Dwyer, Reverend Philip. *The Diocese of Killaloe.* Hodges, Foster and Figgis, Dublin, 1878.

FitzGerald, Reverend P. *The History of the County and City of Limerick*, McKern, Dublin and Limerick, 1826.

Frost, James. *The History and Topography of the County of Clare.* Sealy, Bryers & Walker, Dublin, 1895.

Gleeson, Dermot. *A History of the Diocese of Killaloe*, Gill, Dublin, 1962.

Gleeson, Reverend J. *Cashel of the Kings*, Duffy, Dublin, 1927.

Howard, J. J. and Crisp, F.A. *Visitation of Ireland*, London, 1897-1918.

Lindsay, W. A. *The O'Briens*, London, 1876.

MacLysaght, Edward. *Irish Families*, Figgis, Dublin, 1972.

McCarthy, Joe. *A Brief History of Dromoland Castle*, Dromoland, Co. Clare, 1971.

O'Brien, The Hon. Donough. *History of the O'Briens from Brian Boroimhe, A.D. 1000 to 1945*, Batsford, London, 1949.

O'Brien, Sir Edward, fourth Baronet. *Directions for a Day's Shooting at Dromoland* (circa 1830), Dolmen Press, Dublin, 1961.

O'Brien, Ivar. *O'Brien of Thomond*, Phillimore, England, 1986.

O'Brien, R. G. *Noel (Nova Scotia) amd the Genealogy of the O'Briens*, New Bedford, 1925.

O'Donoghue, John. *Historical Memoir of the O'Briens*, Dublin, 1860.

O'Donovan, John. *Annals of the Kingdom of Ireland by the Four Masters*, Hodges & Smith, Dublin, 1848.

O'Hart, John. *Irish Pedigrees*, Murphy & McCarthy, New York, 1923.

Steele, W. B. *The Parish of Devenish*, Ritchie, Enniskillen, 1937.

Talbot, The Very Reverend M. J. *The Monuments of St Mary's Cathedral, Limerick*, The author, Limerick, 1976.

Touhill, Blanche M. *William Smith O'Brien*, University of Missouri Press, Columbia and London, 1981.

Walsh, Micheline, *Spanish Knights of Irish Origin*, Irish Manuscripts Commission, Dublin, 1965.

Weir, Hugh W. L. *The Royal O'Briens*, Shannon Development, Co. Clare, 1982.

White, The Very Reverend P. *History of Clare and the Dalcassian Clans*, Gill, Dublin, 1893.

Williams, J. D. *History of the Name O'Brien*, Mercier Press, Cork, 1977.

## Some journals containing O'Brien material

*The Other Clare*. Journal of the Shannon Archaeological Society (1977-1988).

*Journals of the Royal Society of Antiquities of Ireland* (1907, 1908).

*North Munster Archaeological Society Journal* (1941).

*Journal of the Cork Historical Society* (1897).

*The Irish Genealogist* (1939, 1953, 1980, 1986).

*The Irish Ancestor Dal gCais* (1970-82).

Inauguration stone, Cashel

# Surname variations of Brian Boru's descendants

| | | | |
|---|---|---|---|
| Bryan | MacBrien | McBrian | O'Brian |
| Bryen | MacBryen | McBrien | O'Brien |
| Brian | | McBryen | O'Bryen |
| Brien | | | |
| Briens | | | |
| Brine | | | |
| Brion | | | |

# Clare Castles in O'Brien hands in 1584

| Castle | Barony | Occupant |
|---|---|---|
| Castlelough | Tallaghnanaspull | Baron of Inchiquin |
| Gleaunadow | Tallaghnanaspull | Turlough O'Brien |
| Castelcattagh | Tallaghnanaspull | Earl of Thomond |
| Formerla | Tallaghnanaspull | Turlough O'Brien |
| Tyreadagh | Tallaghnanaspull | Turlough O'Brien |
| Cnoppogue | Dangan West | Turlough O'Brien |
| Castleton Nemenagh | Dangan West | Brune O'Brien |
| Mughane | Dangan West | Donogh O'Brien |
| Rossmanagher | Dangan West | Earl of Thomond |
| Bunratty | Dangan West | Earl of Thomond |
| Cloymemonegh | Dangan West | Earl of Thomond |
| Drumline | Dangan West | Moriartagh O'Brien |
| Rachavollayne | Dangan West | Donogh O'Brien |
| Carroobrighane | Cloynderlaw | Teige MacConor O'Brien |
| Dunmore | Moyasta | Sir Donnell O'Brien, Kt |
| Dunbeg | Moyasta | Sir Donnell O'Brien, Kt |
| Inisdymon | Tuagh more y Conor | Sir Donel O'Brien |
| Glan | Tuagh more y Conor | Sir Donel O'Brien |
| Ballhanire | Tuagh more y Conor | Sir Donel O'Brien |
| Beancorroe | Tuagh more y Conor | Sir Donel O'Brien |
| Tullagh | Tuagh more y Conor | Sir Donel O'Brien |
| Dinnegoir | Tuagh more y Conor | Sir Donel O'Brien |
| Duagh | Tuagh more y Conor | Sir Donel O'Brien |
| Liscannor | Tuagh more y Conor | Sir Donel O'Brien |
| Inchiquin | Tullagh O'Dea | Baron of Inchiquin |
| Tiremacbryne | Tullagh O'Dea | Mahon MacBrien O'Brien |
| Ballycottry | Tullagh O'Dea | Mahon MacBrien O'Brien |
| Carrowduff | Tullagh O'Dea | Mahon MacBrien O'Brien |

| | | |
|---|---|---|
| Killinbuoy | Tullagh O'Dea | Sir Donel O'Brien |
| Moethrie | Tullagh O'Dea | Earl of Thomond |
| Derryowen | Tullagh O'Dea | Baron of Inchiquin |
| Clonowyne | Tullagh O'Dea | Mahon O'Brien |
| Cloyneshelhearne | Tullagh O'Dea | Dermot O'Brien |
| Owarronaguille | Tullagh O'Dea | Dermot O'Brien |
| Kilkeedy | Tullagh O'Dea | Mahon O'Brien |
| Clonrawde | Clonrawde (Clonroad) | Earl of Thomond |
| Clare | Clonrawde | Earl of Thomond |
| Inish | Clonrawde | Earl of Thomond |
| Killone | Clonrawde | Baron of Inchiquin |
| Ballymacooda | Clonrawde | Baron of Inchiquin |
| Inishacivahny | Clonrawde | Teige MacConor O'Brien |
| Inishdagrome | Clonrawde | Teige MacConor O'Brien |
| Inishnawar | Clonrawde | Teige MacConor O'Brien |
| Moyobreacain | Clonrawde | Baron of Inchiquin |
| Caherrush | Clonrawde | Earl of Thomond |
| Tromra | Clonrawde | Teige MacConoher O'Brien |
| Donogan | Clonrawde | Teige MacMorrogh O'Brien |

## The following Abbeys were also in O'Brien possession

| | |
|---|---|
| Clare | Sir Donel and Teige MacConor O'Brien |
| Killone | Baron of Inchiquin |
| Corcumruadh | Baron of Inchiquin |
| Island Chanons | Earl of Thomond |
| Kilfena | Earl of Thomond |

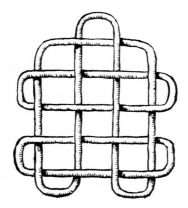

The O'Brien Knot

79

Cratloe Woods, residence of the Stafford O'Briens